A GUIDE FOR LIVING
WITH DEATH AND DYING

Some further books of White Eagle's teaching

BEAUTIFUL ROAD HOME

THE BOOK OF STAR LIGHT

FIRST STEPS ON A SPIRITUAL PATH

FURTHER STEPS ON A SPIRITUAL PATH

THE GENTLE BROTHER

GOLDEN HARVEST

HEAL THYSELF

JESUS TEACHER AND HEALER

THE LIGHT BRINGER

THE LIVING WORD OF ST JOHN

PRAYER, MINDFULNESS AND INNER CHANGE

THE PATH OF THE SOUL

THE QUIET MIND

SPIRITUAL UNFOLDMENT ONE

SPIRITUAL UNFOLDMENT TWO

SPIRITUAL UNFOLDMENT THREE

SPIRITUAL UNFOLDMENT FOUR

THE SOURCE OF ALL OUR STRENGTH

THE STILL VOICE

SUNRISE

TREASURES OF THE MASTER WITHIN

WALKING WITH THE ANGELS

WHITE EAGLE'S LITTLE BOOK OF HEALING COMFORT

WHITE EAGLE ON DIVINE MOTHER, THE
FEMININE, AND THE MYSTERIES

WHITE EAGLE ON FESTIVALS AND CELEBRATIONS

WHITE EAGLE ON THE GREAT SPIRIT

WHITE EAGLE ON INTUITION AND INITIATION

WHITE EAGLE ON LIVING IN HARMONY WITH THE SPIRIT

A GUIDE
FOR *LIVING*
WITH *DEATH*
AND DYING

WHITE EAGLE
with commentary by Anna Hayward

THE WHITE EAGLE PUBLISHING TRUST
NEW LANDS · LISS · HAMPSHIRE · ENGLAND

First published June 2002 as
AWAKENING : A GUIDE FOR LIVING WITH DEATH AND DYING
Corrected edition published under the present title 2006
© The White Eagle Publishing Trust, 2002, 2006

British Library Cataloguing-in-Publication Data
A catalogue record for this book is
available from the British Library

ISBN 0-85487-169-1

Set in Baskerville by the publisher,
and printed and bound in Great Britain
at the University Press, Cambridge

CONTENTS

List of exercises, suggestions for practical action, and a useful reading

Illustration

INTRODUCTION : THE SACRED JOY

HAVE YOU lost a loved one? Are you facing bereavement? Are you trying to come to terms with your own mortality? Do you live with the nagging fear of death? Are you an agnostic, yet a person who longs for reassurance of continued existence? Are you curious as to why so many people believe in things they cannot see? Are you supporting a friend or family member through a critical illness?

If the answer to any of these questions is yes, then this book and the 'guide' of its title, White Eagle, may be for you.

As a generation, we feel both so limited and so knowledgeable. We seem to know so much, and yet we are still mortal, and the unanswerable questions are still those of why we are here and where do we go from here, if we do?

Although it may not immediately be obvious, this book is primarily about consciousness and how we perceive ourselves, our being and our lives. It is therefore very much a book for the living, not just for the dying. It begins with White Eagle's vision of what consciousness actually is, and thus how death is a change in consciousness, rather than an end. In this light, White Eagle talks to us about the true reason for our lives, from a spiritual point of view.

White Eagle is a spiritual guide whose teaching was given through the mediumship of Grace Cooke, and is perhaps best known for the little collection of his sayings, THE QUIET MIND. He always referred to himself as a spokesperson for wise teachers in the world of spirit who are helping humanity onwards in its evolution. These great ones, who have passed through many earthly lives, he says, dedicate themselves to the service of humanity. They offer encouragement and wisdom which has been received through a number of seers and also through ordinary, loving men and women down the ages. Among the many White Eagle books there is another, shorter one for the bereaved, with the title SUNRISE. It will make a very useful companion to this one.

White Eagle has said on a number of occasions, as well as in this book, that one of his main tasks is to help people to overcome their 'mad fear of death'. This book is dedicated to that purpose. It is perhaps no coincidence that the guise in which he comes is that of a Native American. In that culture, anciently and today, there is a sense of total continuation to life, and of very little barrier between one world and the next. His teaching is presented here, I hope, in such a way as to help us make sense of both life and death. The intention is to help provide understanding of bereavement and grief, and to enable the reader in their need to face up to fear and suffering.

I began my career as a teacher and then trained in counselling, but my work also includes teaching yoga. I have used this varied experience in seeking to draw on passages from White Eagle that might reassure you, the reader, of a loved one's continued existence or might make you better equipped to care for a loved one, or deal with grief. It is my hope that White Eagle's words may also dispel fear.

Both my parents are now in spirit, but it was my paternal grandmother's death, when I was twenty-two, which began my own quest for spiritual understanding. We were very close, and in my heart I dedicate my work on this book to her. Her death was something which I had always dreaded. She also died in pitiful circumstances, after a long and humiliating stay in hospital, somewhere she desperately hated being. I could not make sense of her death at all, and indeed my subsequent MA degree in education, which was existentially based, began with a poem about my inability to come to terms with her death.

I read extensively on this subject, but it was a period of panic attacks, brought on by my first visit to the ancient Cathar stronghold of Montségur in France (which I refer to again in chapter VI on suffering), which brought me to a point where I began to look elsewhere for guidance. I began to meditate, and eventually to realise within, a deeper consciousness in which I knew she was still 'alive'. Such inward experiences have done much to change not only how I think about death, but who I am.

Interspersed in the text are accounts from other individuals of their experiences of near-death, caring for the dying, along with descriptions of evidence they have received after the death of their loved ones. All of these tell wonderful stories which may offer inspiration; I hope the experiences I have just described show that this is not necessarily achieved easily. Suffering is real, and while it can be transcended this can often take time.

The book ends with an affirmation of what life really is, according to White Eagle. He describes it as ever-expanding consciousness: consciousness that is limitless, eternal, and supported by a divine intelligence which is loving in a way far beyond our present restricted conception.

The world of spiritual life is not geographically far away from you. It is within you, it is within your own consciousness. We come to help you to expand your consciousness to that world of light which is interpenetrating your physical world. It is a mistake to separate the levels of life by saying, 'We are down here on the earth, and heaven is up there'. We want you to grow in consciousness of this interpenetration of the higher worlds. When we describe to you, for example, a Temple of Healing, we are taking you into the consciousness of such a temple. You are not going 'up there', or 'over there', you are going inward into your spiritual consciousness and, in that spiritual consciousness, you are able to touch infinity and eternity.

We call them higher worlds not because they are set apart from you, above, but because they are light worlds. They are not to be found in the dense material consciousness. But they are instantly to be found when you open yourself in love. By feeling love and compassion for all human beings, you immediately open the gateway to that fuller consciousness of a spiritual state of life. You can find communion with that centre of light.

The previous passage, as the reader may have noticed, is set in larger type. We have done this consistently for White Eagle's words, as opposed to my own, which are in the present size. I should like to acknowledge the help of all those dear to me who have passed into the world of light, and have been with me as I compiled this book. Also, I thank my editor, Colum Hayward, without whose scrutiny the book would be the poorer; Kärin Baltzell, who assisted him; our proofreader, Jacqueline Power; and all those who have contributed their stories to make the book more rich in human experience. I am also grateful to Pat Rodegast and the publisher, Bantam Books, for permission to use an extract from EM-MANUEL'S BOOK III: WHAT IS AN ANGEL DOING HERE?

'Brotherhood' in the text implies not only a community of men and women, but generally all creation as well. 'Master' implies either sex too. Along with some derivatives, these are the only words that resist our intention to offer a text which is gender-neutral.

I hope that this book will help to expand the reader's awareness into realms beyond the physical, through the wisdom and vision White Eagle gives in his teaching. I hope it will help those who are in need of faith and encouragement. Furthermore, I hope that White Eagle's teaching will not only open the mind to the greater life, but touch the heart, and thereby allow the divine spirit to impress the reader with an inner knowledge of the truth of eternal life.

Anna Hayward
April 2002

PART ONE : LIFE

I. A QUESTION OF CONSCIOUSNESS

IF SOMEONE were to ask the question, 'Where are you?', you might answer it by referring to your house, your country, or where you feel you are in your life. But what if they were to be more specific? 'Where are you located within?'. Many people would, on reflection, feel that they are located in their head, possibly somewhere between the eyes. Occasionally, and especially if they were going through an emotional crisis, someone might locate themselves in the solar plexus, or the heart. People who practise yoga, or who are involved in demanding physical pursuits which use their whole body, might locate themselves in every cell of the body, or they might say they are their body as a whole.

Where are you at those times when you feel most alive? Some people might say that at those times they are, at one and the same time, both acutely aware of their body and also soaring above it. Does that make sense? As a yoga teacher, I can certainly agree with this. Doing the postures means that yoga practitioners learn to become aware, eventually, of the minutest part of themselves and of feeling in places where they would not normally be conscious. Practising exercises such as these, one can seem to be connected with all life and in everything, not just the body. It is possible to become aware of a part of oneself which is beyond the body, but also interpenetrating it at a sub-cellular, awareness level. In fact, we become aware that consciousness can take us into places we never dreamt of, simply by becoming aware of the existence of them.

This is what happens in imaginative meditation. Through our imagi-nation we may be able to touch realms which are supernal, and at that moment we can realize that we have an existence which does not only function in the room where we are sitting and the body we inhabit, but extends beyond. This realization moves us towards understanding that all existence is a question of consciousness. White Eagle says:

We wish to put before you certain truths, which you can afterwards prove for yourselves. One of these truths is the fact of a spiritual law ever guiding and controlling the existence of each one of you. Remember that life is *consciousness*. As you grow and evolve, you are expanding your consciousness. The extent of your spiritual power is the extent of your consciousness of higher realms of life, your conscious acceptance of new heights and depths and breadths, of a fuller, richer and more abundant life.

So, in the degree you become more conscious of the smallest details, both in human life and in the world of nature, so you will begin to expand, grow and evolve. This expansion, however, depends entirely upon individual actions and reactions to life. Through actual experience you grow, and eternal life is dependent upon the spiritual quality of the consciousness in you.

Once this is clearly understood, each one of you will so live that you are all the time endeavouring to expand your consciousness of God. By living thus you increase within you the Christ light, which will shine through your life and through your attitude to all the circumstances in your life. For every experience, small or great, sweet or bitter, is intended to give you a further opportunity to expand your consciousness.

Returning consciousness

White Eagle teaches us that life—all life, whether on earth or at other levels—is a process of returning more and more into a complete consciousness, one which functions on all levels of life and comprehends them all. We return to awareness of our consciousness on the physical plane as we are born again in matter. We return to awareness of layers of broader consciousness than the physical when we die. However, our main purpose is to return to an awareness of spiritual consciousness throughout all our being and at all levels.

During earthly life we are often unaware of having any conscious-ness at all at a spiritual level, and so we fear to die. However, in dying we reconnect to a much more alive part of ourselves than we know while on earth. This is why spiritual teachers like White Eagle promote meditation, contemplation, prayer, entering the silence and mindfulness. They know that if we can get a glimpse of our own spiritual level of consciousness while on earth, it will transform our lives from fear to trust. This is the subject of the first part of this book. When we trust, we will touch that fountain of Christ love within our selves. That Christ love is a never-end-ing source of strength and wisdom, and a spontaneous outpouring of kindness and love towards all life.

Soul and spirit

The passages to come are included to let White Eagle himself clarify at the outset the terms 'soul and spirit', and show how they relate to the physical body. White Eagle also defines these terms very beautifully in the first chapter of THE LIVING WORD OF ST JOHN. In St John's Gospel itself is to be found one of the phrases which most opens the door on what White Eagle says here, *In my Father's house are many mansions.*

In order to expand our consciousness to the extent whereby we become completely aware on all levels, we need different 'vehicles' to exist in, and at different stages of our development. Instead of his word 'vehicles' we might easily say 'bodies', but the word 'body' tends to give a limited vision and to suggest the physical form primarily, in a way that is not re-ally appropriate. Actually, our consciousness is housed in many different 'mansions' as our evolution progresses. One might better say that we are usually only aware of one 'vehicle' at a time, the one in which we then reside—whereas we in fact exist, largely unconsciously, in them all.

In the following teaching White Eagle describes the interpenetration of all the forms in which we exist:

The soul is not the spirit. The soul is the temple or the body which you build for yourself during physical life. You are creating that soul through human experience. It is that soul which is your body after death. But the spirit—that is a different matter altogether! It can never die because spirit is eternal with the Father–Mother.

The soul consciousness resides in the head, in the brain; while the spirit has its home in the heart. The soul is the consciousness and expression; the spirit is the divine urge, the infinitesimal ray from the Divine. An ancient symbol of the spirit displayed the heart from which the flame was issuing, which clearly shows spirit as the divine urge—urging each one upwards towards his or her home. God is spirit. Spirit is the light, the ray within the heart which urges a person to aspire to the love-essence of life.

Let us further define spirit and soul. In the past the Wise Ones would teach their pupil that when functioning on the lower triangle (in which you will find the lower organs, the generative organs of the human body) he or she was solely a materialist; when functioning in the head centre he or she was an 'intellectualist'; and when he or she was functioning in the heart centre then that person was an initiate. A materialist, an intellectualist, and an initiate or mystic: here we have a clear picture of the threefold being of everyone that walks this path of unfoldment. The soul consciousness, as we have already said, resides in the head, in the brain; the spirit has its home in the heart. The soul is the consciousness and expression; the spirit is the divine urge, the infinitesimal ray from the divine.

It might also be helpful to explain right away what White Eagle means by 'higher self', in relation to the more limited self of earth. The limited self of earth is the physical body, the 'vehicle' in which each exists while on earth, but this body is not just the material form. It includes the emotions and mind as well. The higher self, then, is the part of us which is aware at a spiritual level—the part which is eternal, and forever linked with the Great Spirit. Our higher self is synonymous with our spirit, and the soul is another 'vehicle' through which the spirit manifests, but on other planes of existence as well as the physical. The soul is actually created by all our lives on earth.

On this subject, White Eagle was once asked, 'Does not the very highest part of us always remain in the higher spheres? And he replied, 'The higher self, the higher soul, is in the spheres, but the life-force, the ray, is in the heart—or you would not be here'.

The tip of the triangle

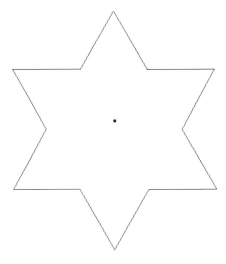

One of the symbols—it is actually far more than just a symbol—which White Eagle has given us is that of a six-pointed star, made up of two interpenetrating equilateral triangles, matching the seven-chakra system of the body (for which see below, p. 53n; the seventh point is at the centre of the star). This is one of his descriptions about the star, which he uses to help us understand what we are:

Let us turn to the six-pointed star, which is formed from the double triangle. The lower triangle represents the lower aspect of a person aspiring to heaven or to God. The higher represents the descent of the three principles, wisdom, love and power (the higher aspects of each person), which then interpenetrate the lower, or material aspect. Spirit interpenetrates matter, and so is formed the double triangle, or Solomon's Seal. However, all the inside part of those interlaced triangles is filled in, and we get the perfect six-pointed star—the realization of the complete interpenetration of God and matter. The star can also be discerned as a symbol of power, because by full interpenetration of the lower by the higher we gain poise and self-mastery.

Soul is the individuality, the individual consciousness, that part of a person which finds expression through the mind. The soul does not incarnate in entirety. I have given you the symbol of the triangle. Recall the triangle on its apex, coming down into the triangle resting on its base; the two of which, when interpenetrated, signify the spirit manifesting in matter. Visualize the triangle descending with only the point penetrating the life of a person. So we find that the greater part of the triangle remains in the higher realms, in its spiritual home. The greater self has not entered into physical consciousness, but only the apex is in contact with the brain of a man or woman.

I hope that will give you some food for thought. In sleep state, when the little point is withdrawn and functions in entirety on the higher planes, it can review the whole history of itself. Therefore often during sleep state memories of past lives recur.

The purpose of your development and growth is that you may learn to function completely. That is to say, that you may bring through not only the point of the triangle, but the whole being, so that your full consciousness can function through the mind and the brain.

The great initiator, death, is the process by which the little bit returns to the greater self. When death comes along, and the little part returns to the greater self, then there follows complete illumination. But the ultimate purpose of life and evolution is that, without death intervening, in time there will come a complete illumination of the soul through the medium of the intelligence and mind consciousness.

Quality of consciousness

There is much scientific debate at the moment about the nature of our universe—how old it is, how vast it is, how unique it is, and how it is composed—and scientists are causing our horizons to expand more and more, physically and mathematically. When one thinks of outer space as we actually see it—perhaps represented on the television, as it appears through a telescope, or when standing under the great arc of sky on a starry night—it is still no easier for us to conceive what the scientists tell us. For example, how can our minds convince us that there are countless trillions of stars and galaxies, that the universe is probably still expanding, that the heart of our universe could be a black hole, that we are standing on just a relatively small lump of rock hurtling round the star we call the sun at nearly 67,000 miles an hour? By a kind of faith we accept all this, and that the only thing that is holding us in place is our speed of rotation of over 1,000 mph. Another piece of trust reminds us that all that is keeping us alive is a layer of air a few miles thick!

Sensorily, we are definitely limited in our perception of life. Scientists tell us that, mathematically, they have calculated that there are many more dimensions than the three or four we once thought, none of which, at the moment, we can experience with our senses! Where are they? Whether or not we see it in this known system, is it actually now so very hard to conceive of a heaven beyond the physical senses, senses which are bound to three-dimensional space and time? Or might not heaven be within, as so many mystics, philosophers and teachers tell us—a state of awareness beyond our daily state of consciousness, not obviously accessible from the material, sensory standpoint, but available to us through different means?

What is intriguing is that a part of us *does* perceive these things. It is not our reasoning mind, but something *felt*, perhaps more in the heart—by a sixth sense—than in the head.

I hope that the idea of heaven being within is not a confusing and disturbing thought, because we know what it is like in there! 'Within' is often a place of confused and difficult emotions; of rambling and upsetting thoughts; of sudden conflicting feelings and unknown bodily reactions that cause us pain. Not exactly Elysian! As the book proceeds, I hope the distinction between what is within in the ordinary sense, and what is within in the deeper sense, will become clear.

We are also told that we are only using—as far as the scientists can tell—a fraction of the brain. What is the rest used for? Could it be in touch with that deeper awareness of which heaven is a part? There are certainly things around us which we cannot experience with the usual range of our physical senses: waves of light, for example; waves of magnetism and radio; sounds too high or low to register; things we cannot see because they move too fast. Might not the human body and mind be only the visible, earthly part of a greater whole which surrounds and interpenetrates it, and which gives it life, and some part of which survives death?

These are of course my own personal speculations, but they may just open out the consciousness in a way which makes it easier to understand the book. Continuing with the thought, the question then is what the earthly existence and the non-earthly part mean to each other. In realising what *we are*, we may also become aware of what 'heaven' is. Spiritual teachers like White Eagle come to remind us of who we are, which we may have temporarily forgotten. They remind us too of what we are seeking to achieve through incarnating in matter. However, those who love us in the world of light, and whose awareness is greater than ours, know that from their higher perspective it is not so much that we live (for life is eternal) but *how* we live which matters. Life on earth is precious for many reasons, not least of which is the rich ground it offers for soul development.

Men and women make such a mistake when they think of heaven as remote, as far beyond their attainment. Heaven is within you, and your spiritual aim is to learn to find heaven within, while you are still in a physical body. Then you will go to a heavenly state when you slip off your coat of skin. Death is an initiation. It can initiate the soul into degrees of life which are either lower, intermediate, or higher. This depends upon the state or the quality of your consciousness while you are living on earth.

What awakens and quickens the divine spirit in you? The answer is simple. It is human experience. The only way for any soul to awaken to the divine or Christ consciousness is through its own experiences, its own feelings, even through its emotional, mental and spiritual suffering.

This awakening is precisely what happens to souls that pass over to the next life who have been loving to others. They may not be highly educated or know a great deal intellectually, but their hearts have found the key to heaven, because on earth they fraternised with and did not exploit or patronize their fellow men and women, and accordingly entered into their joys and sorrows with them.

To illuminate this process, I have in mind a young man who may not have been very religious. Indeed, his only religion was his kindness. When he awakened over here in the spirit life, he was astounded, for his soul at once realized light, happiness, serenity. There was no death for him. There can be no death for anyone who has learnt to love all human beings, and also to love and protect the animal kingdom. All nature shall be ruled, and indeed will some day be governed, by the divine law of harmony and love.

When you see a display of selfishness, try to be tolerant, and see not only selfishness in your brethren, but a striving of the higher self for expression. See in them the higher self which will, one day, shine forth and make a powerful, radiant soul. All the faults in human kind can be seen from a different angle, which is perhaps why our beloved elder brethren and masters are always compassionate, never judging. Spirit communicators are only simple human beings, but have a measure of illumination, a measure of brotherhood in their hearts, and see beyond the dark veil of materialism. They see beyond the veil which hides you from truly understanding your companion, your brother or sister on earth.

What we are trying to show you is that within yourself you have all knowledge; that the life within you is conscious of everything. What you, and all people, are learning when you incarnate into a physical body is to expand that consciousness of yours—which is your life. This is the sole purpose of being.

What the Master taught us

During his ministry the master Jesus, or the Great Initiate, as White Eagle sometimes calls him, often talked allegorically. Great writers and speakers have frequently presented the complexity and depth of life in stories, and have used imagery and symbols to give a picture and a feeling of what they are trying to present. They thus acknowledge, as Jesus did, that a language, rooted in three-dimensional matter and linear time, is not sufficient to the task of conveying the spirit of life.

The next sections, namely 'What the Master taught us', 'The master within—living the truth', and 'The raising of Lazarus—the real awakening', all contain passages from White Eagle on subjects which Jesus covered relating to the spirit, death of the physical body and resurrection. In all of these he is trying to help us understand the depth of Jesus' allegorical teaching on eternal life, and to bring to our attention the real purpose of that teaching—not so much to remind us that life is eternal, but to show us how to live, and why we live, and seem to die.

The idea of 'the Comforter' comes from St John's Gospel, chapter fourteen and after, and is taken up further in chapter IX of this book.

The purpose of your life is that you may live in the spirit and
that the Divine Breath may live in you; and that as you climb the
ladder or the arc of life you may take with you an individualized
soul, pure and true. Thus you can enter the kingdom of heaven
as a living soul.

Some confusion may still exist about what is spirit. We will
try to make clear what we mean by spirit. Because people are
said to be possessed by spirits and Jesus is said to have cast out
unclean spirits, the word 'spirit' may have more than one meaning. The true meaning of spirit is the Holy Breath. Spirit is
sometimes called and actually is life; but an animal kind of life
which is largely automatic is not the life of the spirit—it belongs
to the physical world. Life which is eternal is not of this world.
Jesus said, *The prince of this world cometh, and hath nothing in me.* The
prince, the ruler of this world, the being who directs the physical
aspect of life, has nothing, no hold on life, in real spirit. It is not
the breath or divine essence of life. It seems necessary to make
very clear the difference between pure spirit and life confined
to physical matter.

To give some indication of what it may mean when this pure
spirit is born again into the soul of a person, let us consider
something which takes place when two people become separated
through death. One continues in the world; the soul of the other
goes onward. Perhaps there comes a wonderful experience for
the one that is left, whose soul is raised in consciousness to the
plane of spiritual life where the loved one now dwells. Some
of you may even have experienced this great wonder, this true
communion, this at-one-ment, this attunement of spirit. Or it
may be that in the quiet of meditation you have touched for
a flash—you could not hold it long—the cosmic or the Christ
consciousness, and been aware of the plane of pure spirit. No-
one who has experienced this can ever forget it.

This is what Jesus had in mind when He spoke to His disciples about the necessity for Him to leave them before they could receive the spirit of truth, the Comforter. He knew that they were clinging to His physical presence. This is comparable with how some people look at spirit. A number of them get to know spiritual truth *intellectually*. They contemplate with their mind, they meditate upon, they think ever intellectual truth. They acquire a scientific spiritual knowledge.

Jesus often taught His disciples. Many of them had been with Him a long time. He knew that much He said was only understood intellectually as far as they were concerned. It had not penetrated deeper than the intellect. Yet what a vast difference there is between merely knowing things and becoming spiritually a part of life!—or in other words receiving into the soul the divine breath, which is pure love: not a love which is passionate or emotional but one which is pure. Such a love is the act of giving. If love gives, it must in turn receive: it is the law. You cannot give without receiving, but *it is more blessed to give than to receive*.

Why did Jesus say this? Because without first learning to give it is impossible to receive. To receive what? To receive the Comforter. The spirit of truth is the Comforter and this spirit cannot be received (or welcomed) by the soul until it has learned to feel the impetus of love so strongly within that it can only spontaneously give and give and give.

Many live only in the physical body and think that physical things are the most important; even when they know of spiritual matters they still think the former to be the most important. In a degree they are right: physical life is important because it enables the soul to meet experiences which can quicken the breath of life within it.

The ideal for us all is to place physical life in correct perspective. Physical life forms only a part of life; it is not the whole.

Moreover, physical life in itself cannot live eternally. The body dies, but the Holy Breath can impregnate the soul which the seed creates for itself out of its own desire nature; and that Holy Breath is eternal. Once received into the soul it brings a stimulus and the soul attracts to itself from the physical plane of life all that is most lovely in creation.

Another thing Jesus said to his disciples was, *Whither I go, thou canst not follow me now.* What did he mean? Those of you who believe in life after death will be puzzled, for if he referred to the spirit world we must all in due course follow him. Remember that he could see into the minds of his disciples and knew much of his teaching was only intellectually understood. Therefore he knew that until something happened to shake them, to wake them up to the realities of pure spirit, they could not follow.

It is one matter to know spiritual truth intellectually and quite another to be so clothed in spiritual truth that every thought and word and act is a spontaneous expression of divine love and life. You may say, 'Oh, it is not possible to live like this'. We know your difficulties; but we also know that it is an effort which must be made. You must keep on and on. If you can express even for one flashing moment that spontaneous love, you will have taken a momentous step forward.

The master within—living the truth

The following is White Eagle's commentary on a very human story from St John's Gospel (chapter XXI). It is taken from the book, THE LIVING WORD OF ST JOHN, and is a story about the reaction of his disciples after he was crucified. It describes how, grieving, they were out in a boat fishing when, in his resurrected body, he came to them. 'Remember', says White Eagle, that the disciples 'had undergone a terrible ordeal; they had seen their Lord taken and crucified, and it seemed that with all his glory and greatness he could not save himself from his enemies, so the disciples were heartbroken and disillusioned'.

Throughout his ministry, the Master continually made use of the symbols of the bread and the fish. We hope we have made it clear that the resurrection of the body of Jesus did in a sense take place; but that its elements had become so purified by the Christ light and love which had manifested through them that nothing remained to cause decay, as in ordinary death. It was the true body of the arisen Christ that manifested to the disciples.

In spite of all Jesus had taught them, they were still wrapped up in their personal selves, conscious mainly of their physical needs. So when their Master was slain they lost faith, they were back where they had started, with their attention centred on practical things such as a means of livelihood. So often it happens that souls are raised to a state of spiritual ecstasy and then some trouble comes along and faith and belief are shattered, and the heavens seem as brass. It is a major test of their steadfastness and sincerity, and one which they may feel they cannot pass. They say, 'I trusted, believed, and thought I was following the Master, and it did not work; and now everything has gone wrong! I will have nothing more to do with religion'.

This is exactly how the disciples were feeling. So they put to sea to get on with earning their living, unaware that their Master was with them all the time, and that what they really needed was spiritual food. Before, he had been continually sustaining their spirit; now they were left—just as you will be left at some time, just as you will stand alone when your testing comes. What then? Will you follow the spirit or will you return to worldliness?

Jesus bade them cast the net on the right side of the boat—in other words, saying, 'Seek your spiritual food in the right way'. If you work solely for the welfare of the body you will catch nothing; if you seek purely intellectually you will be disappointed. But if you cast your net on the right side, in the right way, your net will be filled to breaking point with all the sustenance you need; yet the net will not break.

Then follows an interesting point. We are told that the master had kindled a fire to cook the fish. As the story is told by John it seems natural enough; the Master was there waiting to receive his friends, having lit a fire wherewith to cook the fish. But do you not understand that this was a spiritual fire (and therefore not earthly fish, either), a divine fire which Christ kindled on behalf of his disciples? In other words he quickened within them the divine fire of love. When their hearts were thus opened, when once the divine fire burned within, then they were ready to receive the food so divinely prepared and made ready for them. Then at last their soul-hunger was satisfied.

The raising of Lazarus—the real awakening

The biblical story of the raising of Lazarus reminds us that in the New Testament Jesus himself was not alone in surviving apparent death. We are awed by the ability Jesus showed in bringing someone back after they had left their body. By this act Jesus demonstrates the tremendous possibilities inherent in mastership over physical matter, and brings us hope that death is not immutable for any of us.

In his interpretation of the biblical story of the raising of Lazarus,* White Eagle presents us with a way of looking beyond the sensation, to the purpose behind this act; a purpose which, yet again, brings spiritual awakening to the forefront of our reason for being, and at the same time shows why the material and earthly reality is of vital importance for this awakening.

*The story of Lazarus forms the bulk of chapter XI of St John's Gospel and like the previous story receives detailed comment in THE LIVING WORD OF ST JOHN, although the present paragraphs are previously unpublished. It is taken up again in the section 'Engage with Life', in chapter II.

This brings us to another subject—the esoteric symbolism of the raising of Lazarus. In this we find an ancient truth manifesting. It is not merely the miracle performed by the Master Jesus that is significant: we touch in this presentation upon teaching which has come down the ages, an experience which every soul must pass through. Through this miracle Jesus sought to show that although a man or woman comes to the earth and reincarnates again and again, nonetheless until the Son or the eternal life becomes quickened within, the soul still sleeps. In successive incarnations the person contacts only the world of illusion, of matter, of 'death'.

We tend to identify ourselves with the being of earth, of the lower plane—in other words, with Lazarus. We tend to identify our natures with the animal nature, but we need to distinguish between what we appear to be—the lower self—and that eternal life, the Son. That life is in us all, and was exemplified for us in the master Jesus' own life.

In the miracle we see the divine life exemplified once more in Lazarus the human being, and God so glorified in human form that the physical body rose from death to life. This miracle not only relates to man and woman in the beginning; but also tells of the soul's final destiny. Then indeed there shall be no beginning and no ending, but one eternal circle. Each soul shall rise when the glory of the eternal life shines forth from the tomb of the dead self, and the dense body will be transmuted from death to life.

Jesus demonstrated this eternal truth by his own resurrection; for what was, what appeared to be, of the physical, was transmuted to the spiritual. The body which rose from the tomb was no body of earth, but created from the spiritual elements. What was of the earth no longer existed.

The beloved Master wept in agony, some said, at the loss of

his friend Lazarus—which shows us that the Master not only felt sorrow as you understand it, since when your friends suffer you also feel the sorrow, but more. The Master identified himself with the actual experience. He filled with sorrow, shared the joy of his friend.

This level of empathy is attained with mastership. And so you will perhaps better understand now why we continually urge you not to spend too much time in reading, however wise the words you may read, but rather to identify yourselves with life, with the joy and the sorrow of humanity....

How can you enter into the depths of human experience unless you at some period of your life become as the least of these human beings, my children? You must have felt the sorrow of the criminal, the utter misery of the woman taken in sin—you must have experienced the crudities of the flesh, the craving of the drunkard.... You must know the utter despair of the outcast, and have suffered with the condemned.

No, do not be too respectable. And do not be amused when we say this. We speak of grave things. My brethren, no man or woman who draws aside from degradation or suffering can yet identify him or herself with the Master. Even at His death, so-called, He was crucified between *thieves*; and it was the woman at the well, the woman in adultery, the publican and the sinner, with whom He identified himself.

Love, my beloved brethren! Love to the very fullest, so that by love you may drink the cup to the very dregs.... Knowing as you do the life and the glory, you cannot live apart and become immersed in self. Be conscious of the increasing growth of divine wisdom, of the beauty of God within. Pray that your human experience, wherever it takes you, will bring compassion and love, until the body of earth die to self and be resurrected to God.

Creating your next life

Throughout the preceding passages White Eagle's comments on Jesus' teaching are designed to point to the fundamental and pivotal place of compassion and love in the development of spiritual consciousness. It is the increasing awareness of the essence of divine love within us which will mean that eventually we need not die in the way we seem to do now. As we realize—that is, make real—for ourselves, through the experiences of our life, that we are loving beings, so that divine spirit will work through the physical form more easily, until the very atoms of the body become spiritualized. It is the love within us and our realization of it which brings mastery over matter. Such is its power, as demonstrated by the Master's own transition.

It follows from this that how we think about life is as important as what we do. All that we are while on earth is registered, including how we think, and is carried over into the afterlife state by our soul body. Then, the next life we have on earth is shaped from that soul body, and thus White Eagle reminds us of the importance of not only acting, but thinking aright.

One of the first steps on the path of spiritual unfoldment is the power to think rightly. Most certainly, as you think, so you become; so you become physically, so your character is developed, so your surroundings are created. These things are seen because they manifest on the physical plane of life; but it is not often recognized that there is another plane upon which you live, to which your thoughts are continually contributing. They are creating the conditions of an invisible yet individual world.

This world is sometimes referred to as the soul world. It is thought, not incorrectly, that the soul is that body which the spirit inhabits or works through or uses in order to contact the physical life through the physical body. A truer conception, though, is to regard the soul as a temple being built in the heavens, or in the invisible world. It is the sum total of the thoughts and the experiences of many lives.

Not only has the individual a soul, but a world has a soul. At the moment we deal with the soul of the individual. The soul body, then, results from the creations of the mind and the actions of the life spent on earth—of each life thus spent. When the physical body is finished with, the soul lives apart from the physical plane, in varying states and conditions, sometimes sleeping, sometimes active. At all events the soul retains the memory of the past in every detail.

Have you thought how wonderful is the memory of the body and the brain, which brings forth into the mind living and vivid pictures of past episodes in your life? Notice that the memories most easily retained are of things which have had a profound effect upon your soul. They are more easily relived. When death takes place (sometimes just before, sometimes immediately after) mental pictures of the life which has passed flash up, as it were, as if the consciousness were a cinema screen.* It is part of your soul development for you to review all the events of your past and consciously to register their effects upon your spirit. Such a registration creates an enduring memory, which Rosicrucian brethren call the seed atom, a memory carried over from life to life in the soul. Thus there dwells within you (and within every one) this seed pocket, or purse of memory. Is it not useful to think of this pocket, or purse, full of the wealth of the past, tucked away inside you? True, in the average life it is not discovered, examined or opened, but it remains, carried over from life to life and added to by each life-episode. Sometimes in dreams that little purse is examined—and what is the result? You have most amazing dreams which are not the result of your conscious state in the present, but are visions which strike a chord of memory.

*This theme is developed further in the section 'The Akashic records', in chapter X.

If you have been interested in your past incarnations you will say, 'I wonder if I lived as that dream depicted'.

This is a vast subject, because all impressions and the thoughts which have ever passed through the mental body are registered in the soul, in this wonderful 'temple' which you are constructing in the heavens. Biblical symbolism refers to this as 'Solomon's Temple' and it is also the 'Temple' of the Masons, the 'Temple' of all esoteric brotherhoods. When it is realized by the individual that all his or her thoughts and experiences go to create this temple, then the material which is yours should be so moulded as to create something worthy and not shameful.

Do not think that even your thoughts are secret, for that which is thought (and prayed) in secret shall be shouted from the housetops. Because people cannot read your thoughts, do not think that thoughts pass and are forgotten and buried. The time will come when you yourself will see your thoughts as living pictures, and even as life itself. You have seen films which have inspired you and made you thankful to be either woman or man, and inspired you to go forth into the world and accomplish something noble and great. Remember then that this is what the soul experiences at some time, somewhere; for you will see yourself and it will be like looking upon a picture.

II. THE LARGER PICTURE

AS WE CAN see from his teaching, White Eagle assures us that there is a purpose behind our lives which goes far beyond death of the physical body. In all his teaching on this subject he seeks to help us take our minds off the death of the earthly form. Instead, he urges us to dwell on that purpose, so that when death comes it is for us simply another part of an awe-inspiring, but totally creative and good, plan. It is part of the divine plan for our reunion, in full consciousness, with a spiritual love so profound that, when the moment comes, we will know the wise purpose behind all we have suffered.

White Eagle was once asked about this outcome. The questioner said, 'To what is humanity coming?' In his reply, White Eagle talked about what he calls the inner teaching (the teaching which is the wisdom of the ages, and underpins all faiths), but also that teaching which we are all aware of inwardly through our intuition. This sort of intuition, he would say, is our higher vision and it is in touch with our spirit and with God.

With the fuller consciousness there will be a change in the physical body. Even now you are beginning to feel it: an etherealization, a development of the body of light. Some are trying to purify the texture of the physical body by abstaining from coarse indulgence, and in this purifying process, begin to feel 'lighter'. Thus there comes a closer permeation of the body of light—the vital body. In time the physical body will become so light and refined that it will have gained regeneration, and no longer know death. It all comes to this; your consciousness is gradually being raised to a plane of universal brotherhood.

Another aspect of what we call inner teaching is knowledge that can be given to you of the invisible eternal life. The inner teaching can tell you of that lovely world to which your soul goes when it is withdrawn from the physical. It will also tell you that you will return again and again until you have learnt to master all the forces which are gently playing upon your life on the physical plane; until you have learnt to discipline yourself in order that you may comprehend these forces; and until the spirit has grown from the tiny seed or the tiny babe has grown into a son–daughter of the living God. This growth comes when you have attained what we of the spirit would call mastership, which means when you have gained full control over all these forces playing upon you. A master knows how to use these forces to perfect his or her body, mind, emotions, and soul. A master knows how to mould this perfect son–daughter of God. When this happens, when you have attained complete control over yourself and the forces around you, you will no longer die.

You may have heard of instances when a master did not die physically but his–her physical body was caught up into heaven. Many would scoff at this idea and say that everyone must die. No, everyone must live, and when the physical form has become perfectly disciplined and is properly treated and trained, it does not get disease and it does not die. Even if there seems to be a disintegration of the body, it is only temporary. The atoms of that body are quickly reassembled. But such a body is then of finer substance. The body of the Christed one, the Adept, is pure and perfect. A holy person is truly a healthy person.

All this inner teaching is to help you to live your life according to the limitations of your karma so that you are transmuting pain and suffering into joy. The messengers come back, and will come back with increasing numbers, and with increasing power to help you to awaken to your own spiritual heritage. Henceforth you may walk on the right path, or what you call 'the straight and narrow way'. The straight and narrow path is not really straight and narrow; it only appears so, because you have to discipline yourself and cannot do just what the lower self wants. Really it is a path of ever-increasing light, a light which beautifies your life—your mind and your emotions and your very physical and material conditions, creating harmony and happiness in them. The spiritual life, the straight and narrow way, leads to heaven, heaven on earth.

You are now living an eternal life, a truth we want to get home to you most carefully. At your present state of evolution, your physical body has to decay and change its form. You will then manifest in a new body which you have been creating for yourselves all the time you have been living in the flesh. A time will come, though, when the full consciousness or wisdom of those in the heavenly life will come to you. Then you will spiritualize every atom of your body, and instead of decaying and dying your body will become illumined and glorified—a fact which Jesus demonstrated so plainly.

People at present are still blind, and they cannot understand the meaning of the resurrection of the body. They argue: 'Oh, it is all wrong. The body cannot be resurrected!'. No, not in its present state, but some day it will no longer decay. Rather it will become purified, rarefied and of course invisible to people at a lower level. So it continues to unfold, this wonderful eternal life, this development, this spiritualization of life, this glorification of the Creator and of His–Her creatures.

We are told that in the beginning was the Word; and that Word was a vibration, a mighty sound which reverberated in a circle. This earth, creation, is that circle, which may expand and expand. We suggest, therefore, that you think of your life as being held in a circle of light in which you are enfolded; that all of you are living within that Word, within this circle of light and power and protection.

One ray of light

As we read what White Eagle has said about consciousness and the purpose of our lives on earth, we begin to get some understanding of the larger picture. Sometimes he says that the purpose of life is to grow into complete consciousness, sometimes that it is to grow in love. The two amount to the same thing, I feel sure. Along with this we are assured of the vital importance of each individual life in terms of our reactions to daily events and the circumstances in which we find ourselves. We are assured also of how these have shaped our present life, and will shape the life to come, both after death, and when next we come back to the earth plane.

However, to some minds, a problem may occur in understanding how we can identify with both spirit and matter. On the one hand, we are asked not to shun matter—to understand its importance and to live all aspects of life, right down to the dregs, if they are presented to us (p. 29). We are asked to understand deeply what love is by living it, and sometimes living without it, as the disciples did. On the other hand, we are asked to remember in our response to life that we are spirit, and that matter is an illusion created for us as a learning experience.

When we are faced with bereavement and our own mortality, then matter and spirit, and their relationship to each other, take on a specially precious significance. The visualization opposite was designed to illustrate how it is possible to conceive of oneself as being limited matter and unlimited spirit simultaneously.

Jesus endeavoured to teach his disciples that there was neither a 'here' nor a 'there'. He showed them that all was present. All was omnipresent, God-ever-present. The etheric, mental, celestial: all these planes interpenetrate. This is hard to understand when you are limited by a mental conception as to the nature of space and time. We tell you from time to time about certain glorious states of consciousness to which you can attain. You are aware that as you sit here you are conscious, if you wish, of your body.

If you want to reach out you can be conscious of your emotional body. That is, your emotions become stirred and your desires active. This quickens the astral state of life, which is governed by feeling, by emotion. Then again you can reach out above the emotions, and by an effort of will become active on the mental plane. You can even go beyond that mental conception when the higher emotions come into operation and you become conscious of a heavenly state. Step by step, in meditation for example, you go through the varying states of consciousness to the mental and the heavenly. When you once reach this state you are still aware of the others; you experience communication between the heavenly consciousness and your body, because you have both stimulated the heavenly consciousness and also linked the heavenly with the earth life. Yet the one life contains all these states of consciousness. All is here; all is present.

A RAY OF LIGHT

Imagine yourself as a ray of light—not *under* a ray, but *as* a ray of light, one which reaches right from the heart of the spiritual sun. It comes from God, right down to the earth. The body you are in is how that ray manifests on earth. All of the ray is just as much you, but it is at this lowest end that it manifests as body. Elsewhere this ray, still you, manifests differently: as pure thought, or as feeling, colour, vibration, or as light, ether, spirit, love.

At the heart of the spiritual Sun from which you come you are as radiant and strong, as brilliant and amazing, as the Sun itself. White Eagle assures us of this. Yet just as a ray of light disperses and becomes weaker the further away it is from the source, so too on earth we are not quite so radiant and wonderful. Nevertheless, you as a ray of light are all these things at the same time. You are not separate from the highest aspect while you are on earth, because you are the whole ray. At the very same moment that you are here in this place, with all the earthly thoughts and feelings, you are also a radiant spirit. Indeed, it is that radiant Christ-spirit which gives life to all the rest—to all of you. Without that you would not exist at all.

White Eagle tells us, 'The one life contains all these states of consciousness'. You are the whole ray of light. So even at the same time as you are the self most encased in matter—most fearful, defensive—you are also the highest of which you can conceive: the noblest, the most heroic, the most loving. Your awareness stretches to states of consciousness which we cannot conceive of with our limited earth mind. And, of course, what is true for you is true for me and true for others also.

Because we exist, or can be aware, at all these levels of consciousness, our life is one of choice at all times. What do we choose to identify with? The noblest, or the most defensive, self? It is not a question of travelling from one to the other, but of what we choose to aspire to be in this moment on earth. We may not always be able to sustain contact with the highest or identify completely with it; we may not feel able fully to let it shine through, but it is always there. Each one of us is always the complete ray of light.

When we are encased in matter it is harder to identify with the spiritual part of ourselves; even to remember it is there. It is hard to choose love. White Eagle puts it this way: 'At many times the spirit is overwhelmed by the conditions in which it finds itself and it creates for itself karma. This karma causes reincarnation. All you can do is to endeavour to keep your vision upon the one grand truth that God is light; that you—the divine spirit—you also are light'. So it takes patience, for the limited self wants that spiritual part to manifest fully all at once. Patience includes keeping the door of possibility always open: knowing that by believing we are this whole ray of light, it will one day be radiant right through into the earthly self.

We can sometimes feel hopeless, as though it will take all eternity to be as we wish to be. It is just like when we have a pain somewhere in our bodies which is so strong we find we cannot take our minds away from it. Sometimes it is so bad that our whole body seems to be in pain. However, at every moment we are infinitely more than that pain, just as we are with feeling or experience which may restrict us.

The key is in remembering, remembering the bright world. But in remembering, we must not despair of ourselves, or of others, if for instance we realize we have been very defensive and negative. As soon as we remember to do so, we can identify once again with the part which is light; and then we are light, no matter what has gone before—because we were never separate from light. All the time we were in darkness, struggling with the limited, defensive self, we were still radiant beings.

More than this, the whole point of our lives is so to identify with the spiritual part of the ray in the exercise, that the whole ray, right down to the earthly level, is as bright as the sun. So every time we remember that other radiant part of ourselves while we are in the middle of the struggle, we bring that radiance into matter. As we think of ourselves, so are. White Eagle talks about states of consciousness, of which thought is one. Therefore our thoughts about ourselves have a life. He encourages us never to give way to despair, or to lack confidence in ourselves, for then we are denying that we are spirit right now. It is what White Eagle calls 'denying the God within'.

Let us come back to the visualized image, of the self as a ray of light. Even where the light is diffuse and weak, it is still light. Within that diffuse light, at the heart centre, is the spark of the Christ-spirit. It is the source of our true radiance during this earthly state of consciousness.

One of the important benefits of meditation is that when, in humility, quietness and love, we open ourselves to the flame of Christ within the profound stillness of the heart, that light is stimulated. The route opens, the route travelled by the ray of the self, right back to that part of the self which knows no limitation and no fear. That spirit of love flows into the heart and mind, feelings and body of earth, reassuring, dissolving the pain; filling the lonely spaces with sweetness and joy. As we become aware of the spiritual self which we are, so we also receive awareness of the spiritual Sun from which we come.

Each of us is a son–daughter of the living God—a ray from His–Her heart—and can never be lost or abandoned, can never be disconnected, can never be less than we truly are. Our whole life is an act of continually remembering this—choosing this awareness—and as soon as we remember, we are no longer bound but free. We are free to be as loving, strong and caring, and as peaceful, gentle and fearless as we really are.

White Eagle says:

When we say there is no such thing as time on the spiritual planes of existence or indeed on earth, you will smile at us; but there is no such limitation, because all time is at this instant. At this very instant you and we are in eternity. All that was or ever will be is existing now.

Your physical world is a world of illusion—it is not what you think it is. Do you realize that your physical world, in reality, is a world of light? It is built of light. Do you know that your physical body, if you could see it with clear vision, is composed of light? God's life and essence permeate every atom of His–Her creation and every vibration of your inner being. Each soul has to learn that all substance is God. It has to learn that everything which seems solid matter is really charged with divine energy and light. If you could live always conscious of this light, you would find that the very atoms of your body would gradually become etherealized. Then you would live for ever more in a body of light. Think along these lines and try to realize that your true state of embodiment is in the eternal light.

Your body has around it a shield of light. This same body of light cannot be seen by ordinary people—that is to say, by people still imprisoned in matter—because they are in exactly the same position as prisoners bolted and barred in a dark cell. We are endeavouring to put profound truth into simple words. What can bring about this change in the physical matter of your body? This divine fire which can be awakened by something finer than itself—literally by the voice of God within your innermost heart. Some would call it the 'I AM' speaking, but remember you need to distinguish between the personal 'I AM' (which is of the earth, earthy), and the divine 'I AM', which is the voice of the living God. The latter is the pure, the humble, the lowly, the gentle, the patient, the kindly voice, just as the voice of Christ is.

All will one day realize that they have always lived and had their being safe in God's life and love; that all their fears were empty, idle fears, and that the real purpose of their earth lives has been to teach them to realize their power of command over the four elements and over all matter by a process of surrender to the Divine Fire of Love—the 'I AM' which is the living and universal Christ in all.

The eternal ocean of life, or how to be patient!

I believe that one of the hardest tests for us once we have seen a vision of a greater life, and one of the reasons we are here on earth, is to be patient with ourselves and with others. We expect too much of ourselves too quickly, because our fine minds can perceive a glimmer of what we could be like, and how the earth could be. As White Eagle mentioned in the section, 'What the Master taught us', 'It is one thing to know spiritual truth intellectually and quite another to be so clothed in spiritual truth that every thought and word and act is a spontaneous expression of divine life and love'. It is one thing to know spiritual truth, and quite another to feel it within so strongly that we are able to live it, even when we are surrounded by the material conditions which cause fear and pain.

In the final section, White Eagle talks about the inconceivable extent of life and progress. He refers to a symbol which I find particularly helpful here, which is the spiral. As we journey through our lives we are travelling up this spiral, to heights which are infinite. On our journey we inevitably pass the same point again and again, yet on a higher ring of the spiral each time. How often have we thought we were beyond some difficult event; that we have overcome some trait which is unhelpful, only to find that we meet it again in a different situation some time later? It has to be so—our spiritual self wishes it thus—so that we become completely and utterly 'clothed in spiritual truth', inside and out.

The idea of the spiral going upwards into infinity may also serve to take away the feeling of constant failure which may dog us as we climb, yet again, out of some difficult emotion or circumstance. It presents us instead with an awareness that life is continually expanding and is creative for good—that the journey is not just as important as the end, but is the end in itself!

Using another metaphor, White Eagle was once asked: 'Might not life be likened to a sea or ocean which seems eternal, and we to waves or to the tides which ebb and flow but are always part of the ocean?'. He replied,

Yes, that is a very good simile. Life is always there, but it does not always manifest in the same conditions, or through the same form of matter. You only know physical matter but there are other forms of life and other planets. Life always is. When you are on the crest of the wave you cannot see what is in the trough. That is true in human experience, but we are also thinking in terms of progress. We are thinking that life goes on and on up the spiral. It is impossible for the finite mind to conceive life in all its fullness, impossible for it to conceive infinity or eternity. Do not think in terms of life and death, because there is no death. Do not think because a door closes that another does not open. You pass from one condition of life to another.

In your material problems never be anxious. Oh, how many times do we have to tell you? When one door closes another instantly opens. The trouble is that you like to have too many doors! You are not patient. You have to learn confidence in the eternal love and precision of the light. When a condition finishes never try to hold on to it. Always move forward.

About a century ago, an impulse came through from those wise ones who are helping humanity from spirit that there was a fresh message to come to the world, a restatement of the simple truth of Spiritualism. This simple truth is that people survive death, that there is no death. The truth is that when a person reaches, while still in the physical body, a certain level of awareness of that power of the spirit—when he or she has reached that awareness—he or she knows that there cannot be any death. *There is no death.*

And this is the message, once again restated, that you have to learn by your own goodness; by the spirit of God within you. You have to learn that you are part of that Infinite Power. You are part of that glorious Power, which is spirit, which animates the whole of life on the physical plane. If the spirit was withdrawn from this planet, it would become a dead planet. But the spirit lives in everything: in people, in beasts, in nature. Man or woman is the agent of that Divine Spirit, because men and women have been given intelligence, a very great deal of intelligence nowadays. And we have reached, or you have reached, a vital stage on the path of evolution; because now you are understanding that division between the lower mind or the mind of the body, the brain, and the Divine Spirit....

Will you try to remember that you are, and everyone is, a tiny spark in that infinite and blazing fire, in that divine fire which is life? You cannot be separated from it, you live and have your being in it. You cannot die because it cannot die. You live for ever eternally in that infinite power of Love.

Now you will say, 'Oh, how we regret this ... to go on for ever and ever. We do not like that idea'. Remember, though: the truth is that your life is in that God-life which is not blinded by time nor space. It just *is*. Can we put it more simply for you, in this way? If you have been very happy on some important occasion in your life—when, for instance, you have touched what for you would be supreme happiness—maybe you have said: 'I wish this could go on and on'. Well, you see, it does: that is the point—happiness is always there. It seems to fade away because you are limited by time. But remember you are consciousness,

consciousness in God, and to you at that level of consciousness there is no time, there is no eternity—you just *are*. Now just enjoy any blessed happiness.

When you understand this, and touch that level of Cosmic consciousness, you no longer have any fear. You certainly do not fear death, because you know there is no death. But whatever you think and live and create by your own thought, and your own reaction to conditions, these things remain with you in your soul. They remain until the time comes when you see the error of this thought and action. And when you do so, you want to change them, in the world of spirit or maybe in the world of physical matter—and this is the process of spiritual evolution.

Scientists are right in this regard—that you are on an evolutionary path; but it is not simply one which is for the species, and concerned only with development of skills and brain in order to survive in a material sense. You and we are all, as individuals, evolving. Throughout many, many lives on earth we are seeking to be able to bring through into our lives all the soul qualities which are ours in the higher levels of consciousness.

One thing to remember, as we use language in attempting to describe these states of consciousness, is that language, also, is only the tip of the triangle of true communication. Language is limited by the experience of earth—by space and time, which are phenomena peculiar to this level of consciousness, but do not exist in others. For you, we have to use words like 'up', 'higher', 'down', 'inner'. Even such words as 'levels' give a partly false impression, because all these conditions are states of consciousness, and the best way to think of them is that they interpenetrate each other. When thinking of your bodies, then—your physical, soul and spirit self—think of them interpenetrating each other, so that you come to a glimpse of how all life is one, and all time is now. Part of the reason why communication between your state of consciousness in physical life and that state of life after 'death' is so difficult is simply the fundamental difference which space and time make to our perception of things.

There are many invisible worlds in which the soul can live. The past, the present and the future are all one, although we can never expect anyone of you mortals to understand, because you are limited by time. But when you function on the spiritual plane, there is no time and no space limitation, and these invisible worlds are open.

Yet as we say so often, you cannot understand time. You think of a thousand years as being a great length of time, you think of the age of your world as being immeasurable. No-one has yet arrived anywhere near the truth regarding the actual age of the earth. Great cycles come and pass, and come and pass—night and day—great cosmic night follows great cosmic day…. Get away from the limitation of time, do not think in terms of years … this will help you to gain patience, won't it? There are those who say to us, 'Oh, I am getting old, White Eagle!' Bless their hearts—all eternity lies before them!

Can you think of life pulsating on … on … on…? Get that vibration, or reality, into the heart of your being and you will know no weariness, and never know death. A transmutation, yes, never death. This is the secret of the masters' eternal youth.

Supporting a loved one through their transition—Agnes

My elderly husband was in hospital for observation, though with a multitude of disabilities and debilities. On his last Saturday, when I arrived at the hospital for my afternoon visit, the matron made a beeline for me and told me, kindly, that they thought my husband had had yet another stroke, and wasn't at all well. When I got to his bedside he was barely conscious. I instinctively put my hand on his heart, and spoke to him. He stroked my hand three times, and then lost consciousness altogether.

I sat with him for twenty-five hours, while it was clear that he was slipping away. I spoke to him, mentally, to wish him well on his impending journey, and to thank him for the fifty-two years we had together. They weren't always easy years. He had been a very sick man for many a year, and though he loved us all dearly, his behaviour towards his nearest and dearest was very often very weird and offensive and sometimes downright cruel. It was symptomatic of the survivor-shame he suffered since thirty-four of his relatives perished in various Nazi concentration camps.

But we had actually managed to work through this, and I most gratefully acknowledged the lesson he taught me: to distinguish his higher self, the purpose and intent of his higher being (I had remembered four previous lives we had together) from the machinations of his personality self— which I felt sure he had chosen, like a hair-shirt, to teach me, in love, this most valuable lesson. I discussed all this with him, mentally, and even managed a few chuckles at the memory of the ridiculous situations his hair-shirt personality (and no doubt mine too!) caused for us both.

He visibly weakened by the hour. I tried to visualize the bridge he had to walk across. Finally, when I knew he had made the transition, I heard him say, quite distinctly, 'I am free now, I am free'. No more struggle, no more hair-shirt, no more debilities, but free to rejoin his higher self, with thanks for the tough opportunities this life had offered him, and a job completed to the best of his abilities. He is free now, he is free!

III. HOW TO PREPARE FOR DEATH BY HOW WE LIVE

WHITE EAGLE helps us to cultivate the awareness of how to live in matter, while at the same time knowing we are not bound by it, regardless of how hard our life is, or how limited our present personality. Thus this chapter is not only about preparation for death in an immediate sense, but about how we can live our lives so that death comes as just another part of a fascinating, liberating journey. We are individual beings of light, White Eagle tells us: beings who can never be contained by the conditions of earth, and can consequently never die. What we think of as death is actually illusion. He says:

There are the two aspects of life. The first is the outer aspect in which a person usually dwells; while the other is the inner or spiritual aspect which comparatively few people comprehend and consciously live. The average person lives mostly for the body and on the material plane of life, sometimes for a number of incarnations. Only occasionally are they shaken up, not exactly into a realization of another world but into a questioning as to whether there is another state of existence. When they are bereaved, or when they are very sick, or find they are in some grave trouble, the attention is then arrested. An individual thinks then of the inner things or the other aspect of life, at any rate for a time. Usually, when all is going well on the material plane, he or she is content. Today, we hope, an increasing number of people are beginning to wake up and search for truth.

He also says that we are not isolated on earth; the different planes he speaks of interpenetrate.

All around are the spirits of illumined souls. Each one of you can be a receiving instrument for light and power from these illumined souls. You may, if you will, open your heart and mind to the influence of your spirit companions in order to receive more knowledge on your path, knowledge which will come to you not only by words but by unfoldment of your soul powers. Do not forget that every day, wherever you are, you are a receiving instrument; remember too that God has given you an inner sense which will enable you to tune your receiver to the good and the true and the beautiful, and by these you will know spirit.

We can see, as doubtless you can also see, the fine razor's edge which you have to walk when you step out upon the spiritual path. You can get confused by contact with the emotional, astral plane, which is largely a plane of illusion. We do not mean that all astral form is false, or that it is merely a figment of your imagination. The astral plane is real, even as the physical plane is thought to be real. Some people believe the latter to be as solid as a rock. Unfortunately the majority of people get so immersed in its rockiness, solidity and hardness, that they become encased by solid matter and this solid matter is all they know.

The physical plane in its present form is transient. Its matter disintegrates and then re-forms. Nothing is really destroyed; but the basic physical substance is not as solid as you think, but is moulded and formed by the power of the Great White Spirit. Life in all its forms is always under the control and command of a Divine Intelligence, of Will, Wisdom and Love: that is, of the threefold Creative Power, the Trinity.

Remember this, you must each one of you turn that handle , let the door fling wide open, and enter then into that true world. For this physical world isn't reality: it is transient, it decays, it passes away, it changes its form. But the world of spirit does not crumble and pass away: it is eternal, it is infinite.

Significantly, White Eagle gave the following message at Easter. As his
message shows, this is a time not of death, but of resurrection.

We have said that you live in magical worlds. Only when your
eyes are opened are you able to see this magic, this beauty of the
unseen life which is waiting to manifest and to bring to humanity beauty beyond all your powers of imagination at present.
Why, even your earth is quickening with magic. Look! Go into
the open spaces, into your own small or large gardens, or walk
in the countryside and observe the magical little green shoots
appearing out of the cold, dark earth. Notice a certain aura of
soft pink light around the black branches of the trees. Use your
sense of smell and notice that already there is a faint perfume of
awakening life. All these things are magical. Imperceptibly the
sap is beginning to rise. One can almost say that a resurrection
is about to take place. We always think that the words, *I am the
resurrection and the life*, have their own magical power. They do not
convey the idea of darkness and death but present a picture of
awakening life. For then we look up into the heavens and with
the vision of the spirit we behold the Christ and all his angels
there. We behold the resurrection and the life made manifest.

From out of darkness comes life, and out of evil comes good.
The darkness of earth holding within its womb the seed of life,
and the magical touch of the Sun, the Christ, reaching down,
touching, embracing Mother Earth, bring forth in due season the
Spring, as a child of that love. Is this not the magic of life both on
the material plane and in the spiritual plane? But unfortunately
the souls of many people are earthbound—held in the bondage
of matter—and are unable to break open their shell until the
magical moment comes.

You must frequently have had similar experiences, when you
have felt imprisoned within what you may call evil days, days

of despair, and unable to break the bonds. Then something magical takes place. You do not know what has happened; but apparently, without any external change, you have felt release, like a little chick breaking out of its shell. Your life is changed. You cannot account for it, but it is as though a great cloud, a weight has been lifted from you. Things which had in the past been obscure become clear. Problems and difficulties for which you seemed to have no answer suddenly answer themselves. But was there any particular change in your earthly conditions? No, but a magic had touched *you*, and the light broke in upon you, and you realized that you had been your own prison without knowing it. There is a time—what the Bible calls the 'acceptable time' —for this magic. You must be hushed and still and must wait for its coming.

What is a miracle? A miracle is a happening which is beyond your understanding, because it is outside known physical laws. We are sure that if you look for miracles you will be surprised to find they are continually happening. We say that in order that you may wield this power of white magic yourselves, in order that you may perform what the world would call miracles, you must be able to recognize the miracles which are happening every moment all around you, miracles which the ordinary man or woman fails to see.

In the previous passages, White Eagle has been endeavouring to explain how these 'two aspects of life' work together: 'the outer aspect in which a person usually dwells ... and the inner or spiritual aspect'; and to draw our attention to the importance of the realization of spirit in matter. This realization comes about equally through our attention to how we live our life, and our regular aspiration to spirit. In other words, it comes through engaging with life and with people in the fullest and most creative ways; and, at the same time, creating opportunities to remember that we are spirit, and to allow that spirit to shine through us more fully. The next two sections deal with these aspects in more detail.

Engage with life

When we are ill, or someone we love is suffering, what we often long for is a miracle such as the raising of Lazarus, mentioned in the previous chapter. What White Eagle tells us is that the Master understood it was not the raising of the physical body which mattered, so much as the raising of the consciousness of Lazarus to a point where love would be so strong in him that he could not die, and that this would be achieved through continuing his earthly life for some time longer. In the next passage, White Eagle reminds us of the importance to our soul of identifying with life completely—of living life in such a way that we do not shun others, or the experiences which life brings. If we are to be able to transcend death completely, we need to be able to bring our loving spirit into every condition, so that we are no longer bound by the earth—not only physically unfettered, but mentally and emotionally liberated too.

By immersing ourselves in life, but in an aware way, we begin to recognize miracles and to understand the power love has to work miracles. Not only can we see that power exhibited by a master, but our own inner Christ spirit of love, which can shine out in every dark situation like a beacon of faith and strength for others, and a magnet for unseen forces to come to our assistance in times of pain. White Eagle seeks to strengthen our resolve to live life to the full, and to explain the need for the experiences we go through on our journey.

For the moment, put from your minds the distracting thoughts of daily life. Having come from an outer world which is noisy and full of turmoil, you will not find it easy to do this, and in any case we would explain that the material, the outer, physical life is of great importance. We say this because many people are inclined to disregard the demands of every day in their search for truth and for God. This is a mistake, because you have had a life on the earth presented to you as a most valuable gift. All the same, you are a spiritual being, and as spirit you have powers to unfold. This is the most important thing to remember. Also, you must not confuse spiritual power with psychic power or force; the latter is only one part of a great whole. The psychic plane is that of the soul, the psyche, and you can receive soul impressions when you have trained yourself to be receptive. So there are gifts to develop there, too. See that they are true and beautiful impressions. Nevertheless, the physical life is still important because your spirit, while clothed in physical matter, sometimes has to grapple with very difficult conditions which strengthen the power of the spirit in matter. These are the spiritual gifts you acquire. You yourself have prepared the conditions in which you now live during your past incarnations; and today, during your present life, you are likewise preparing for your next incarnation. The state of life in which you find yourself today is planned by perfect law to ensure your continuing development and growth.

This idea may not seem very acceptable to you, but we want you to understand the importance both of your daily life and your present reactions to all the conditions of that daily life. If they seem unpleasant, try and find out why, and you will perhaps realize that something in you needs discipline and correction. Therefore you are placed in the very conditions that your spirit and your soul most needs to—shall we say—rub off the rough corners. The old mystery schools said that every person was like a rough stone ashlar, and life's purpose was to rub off all the rough places and make the rough ashlar into a smooth stone or cube, ready to be used in the building of a great temple. Your daily life, therefore, is preparing you to take your place in that building. You may think, if you like, of your every incarnation as preparing yet another stone for that purpose.

THE CHARACTERISTICS AND PURPOSE OF
WHITE EAGLE'S FORM OF MEDITATION

ASPIRATION

One of the keynotes of this form of meditation is that it begins with aspiration to God—to the greatest source of all goodness, love, wisdom and creative power that we can conceive. This then raises the consciousness not only above the earthly level, but also above the tumult of the astral and lower mental levels of life, which surround the physical. This highest aspiration connects us with the spiritual spheres.

So one might begin a time of meditation with a piece of inspiring music, or a reading from White Eagle, which will give the opportunity to turn thoughts and feelings away from the worries and distress of physical life. In so doing, we bring our vibration towards a place of harmony and spiritual aspiration.

ALIGNING THE BODY WITH THE SPIRIT

Along with this relaxation of the mind and emotions comes an awareness of how the body is positioned, in order to maximize the aspiration. White Eagle suggests sitting with the spine straight so that the chakras* are aligned and the will is strengthened. The body needs to remain firmly and safely earthed. The meditator is seeking neither to leave the body, to experience astral projection, nor to have occult experiences. The meditator's ideal is to seek communion with God.

USING THE BREATH

The meditator also seeks to create a condition of stillness and peace of mind, body and emotions. This might be achieved by rhythmic 'God-breathing'—an awareness of breathing in not only air, but the spiritual life-force, and with each out-breath attempting to surrender the earthly self and concerns.

---

*The seven chakras were mentioned in chapter I, on p 17. They are centres in the etheric body (that part of the soul closest to earth vibration) which correspond with parts of the physical body: the crown, the brow, the throat, the heart, the solar plexus, the spleen and the base of the spine. At these points the spiritual energy—the vibration—of the etheric body can most easily have an effect upon the physical being. These centres or chakras can therefore be activated when we are meditating.

VISUALIZATION

In meditation we are asked not only to aspire towards spiritual things, but to visualize them as well—to create an image in our minds which, in its loveliness and loving purpose, will form a bridge. This bridge is then the means by which the meditator is enabled to raise their vibration to the higher levels, and is the means by which that inner world may become manifest.

CREATING THE FOCAL POINT

The meditator imagines a focal point for their awareness. This could be as simple as a still white flame, or a rose opening in the light of the sun. Focusing on such an image helps the mind, body and emotions to be brought to a point of stillness and poise. The image itself often evokes a spiritual response, albeit subtle and often unconscious, in the meditator.

THE CONSCIOUSNESS IS RAISED

In all these ways your consciousness is being raised, or heightened. Another way of putting it is that your whole vibration is being raised; your brain waves are changing—and thus you are becoming more receptive to the subtle, higher energies of the spiritual consciousness.

In such a state the meditator can begin to function on a different level—to use senses which are the equivalent of the earthly senses, but on a higher octave, so to speak. Through them, you can experience the spiritual world while still on earth. From the focal point at the beginning of the meditation, other images, feelings and awarenesses may evolve, particularly as you become more experienced in being still and receptive. It is thus that you can catch glimpses of past lives; make a true contact with those in spirit; and be reminded of the spiritual wisdom, power and love which guides and guards us all. Even by remaining focused on the initial image you can find that deeper feelings of peace and clarity, for example, begin to be present. You are becoming spiritually aware, and thus transcending the limits of the earthly personality.

TRANSFORMATION

This contact, no matter how fleeting, is transforming. Not only does it consciously remind us why we are here, and help the meditator to make sense of their life, but it helps and encourages us to live lovingly and creatively for good. A true contact with the spiritual spheres of existence is wholly good and constructive, since the first aspiration has been towards God.

From the first moment a person aspires to meditate in this way, no matter how limited their 'success' appears to be, things are changed within them. A person may not see or feel any differently at first; it may be hard to visualize, or to trust the imagination; it may be difficult to sit still, and to keep the mind focused gently on the image. Nevertheless, the change in vibration and consciousness begins to happen because of the meditator's aspirations, and their desire to raise their thoughts and feelings to a place of true beauty, wisdom and peace. The very thought is enough, which may be one reason why there are so many reports of people spontaneously experiencing meditative states while out in nature, when their minds and feelings are lifted by the scenes they witness.

SERVICE

White Eagle meditation always involves some aspect of service. In a simple way one might use the adage 'as you give, so you receive' to explain it. White Eagle tells us that this statement is a 'spiritual law of life'. But it is not in order to receive that a meditator sends out loving thoughts and light to those in need; rather, it spontaneously happens! When someone who is meditating 'touches' the spirit, that person is reconnected with unconditional love and the deepest compassion for suffering in any form. It is then that they long to give, to bring healing and peace, to bring light into the dark corners of the world. In this form of meditation, therefore, White Eagle teaches us how to send out the light of the Christ star. It is a way of channelling that natural and spontaneous feeling of love so that it can be used for good.

COMPLETION

At the end of the meditation the meditator needs to come back to earthly consciousness in a gentle way, but firmly. The meditator is taught how to seal the chakras, which become more receptive while meditating, so that the person does not feel overly sensitive while going about their daily life. Through this spiritual contact someone who meditates may learn not only that he or she is more than just this earthly being, but also the *importance* of earthly existence, and of living life thankfully, and to the full.

Meditation

Meditation, if entered into wisely, can be the means to integrate the earthly self and experiences with the spirit and soul needs. The following personal account will, I hope, demonstrate what the practice of meditation and prayer can do for us:

Once, in meditation, during the time when I was compiling this book, I was shown some scenes from past lives which all seemed to be illustrating courage and confidence. The last one of these was from a life in very ancient Egypt, when I was undergoing an initiation test. I was being asked to step into a sarcophagus and the lid was being placed on top. As I stepped in, my training took over. The small frisson of fear which I had felt on seeing the test disappeared. What I saw, as I stepped into the sarcophagus, and as the lid was placed over the top, was simply light. Light through all the stone and through all of myself, so that I knew that nothing could contain me because I was in, and of, that light, and therefore beyond any physical box. The test was over immediately.

The meditation reminded me that nothing can contain and limit the spirit, and that spirit is here and part of me now. Even while on earth, with all the restrictions imposed by earthly things (including emotions, fears, thoughts, other people, space, time, bodily limitations, work, culture, my own personal history), nothing can contain me if I am able to identify with my inner spirit.

During the meditation I was in touch with a part of myself which knew that truth very well in those days, but which is not so evident in my present personality! But I felt again what my soul knows, and it was transforming. I knew again the sense of freedom from all conditions, even as they are going on, and the result was intense joy!

We may not always see visions, or past lives, but we are, for a while, in touch with our soul and spirit, and that contact, whether we realize it or not, is influencing our daily thoughts and feelings. I have come to realize more and more each time I practice the form of meditation White Eagle has given us, that a bit of my soul's understanding is penetrating physical matter and my present individuality. What understanding I gain in meditation raises the consciousness of all while also developing my own self-awareness. This meditative state is one which White Eagle encourages us to develop, not only in meditation itself, but constantly. In the following passages he explains how this can be achieved without wandering around in a dream! The first paragraph is taken from the book MEDITATION, in which Grace Cooke introduces much of his teaching on the subject.

When the will to become Christlike grows strong in the heart, it causes an opening in the consciousness for the greater self to descend into the physical body. You think that your physical body is you, but it is only an infinitesimal part of you. If you would contact your true self, go into a place of quiet to commune with your Creator in your heart. Then you will rise in consciousness. That great Light to which you rise is, you will find, the divine self; you, yourself, your own divinity, the real you. By opening your consciousness to this divine self all your vibrations will be quickened and your body will become purified.

Visualization, coupled with devotion and aspiration, will bring the true communion between you and God. It is difficult to put into words what is a state of consciousness, or an experience which takes place in the heart. When you have reached that place you will find an expansion of consciousness, so that you become aware of all spheres of life. You will become at one with the Eternal Spirit, and past and present and future will be one to you. You will be living in eternity. You will recognize, while still living in the body, the difference between yourself, your real self, and this bodily shell.

It should be remembered that the first step towards meditation is sincere worship of and devotion to the Great Light. This particular method of meditation is designed to encourage the growth and expansion of the Christ light in the human heart. During meditation, persevere with the practice of dwelling on the enfolding love of the spirit of Christ. Search for that spark of light within yourself, for this will surely shine amidst the darkness. If necessary, use your power of imagery in order to create this light in your consciousness.

Meditate upon the Sun. Imagine that blazing, golden Sun. This immediately raises you up from the greyness of the earth to the glory of the heavens; that picture you are creating or imagining is part of you. You are part of heaven. You are part of God. The spiritual is more real than your physical life. You touch your chair, you feel with your physical body, and because you feel with the sense of touch you think that you touch reality, forgetting that in a few years all these things return to nothingness. But what you use on the inner planes, the planes of spirit, will live when all around has passed, when the form that you know today is gone. The real things are those which come from your inner self, from the 'knowing' within you. The 'knower' is the real, the true, the higher self, which knows truth.

Gradually, through this process of meditation, we may begin to be aware of two levels of consciousness. There is the everyday level of awareness, in which we go about our daily affairs, and engage with people, sometimes in very earthy, yet enjoyable ways, and then there is the realization that we are also something more than this earthly body, mind and emotions, which we touch during meditation. We may begin to feel this spirit underpinning our earthly life with a spiritual joy and love which is not related to earthly pleasures, although it does have the power to transform them.

Never do we need this awareness more than when we are facing our own pain and mortality, or the suffering or death of a loved one. Then we need the strength and understanding which comes from our spiritual contact: both to make sense of what is happening, and to help us find the resources to see it through. Is it possible that we ordinary folk can find something which will help at such times? Yes, it is. Those people

whose lives we stand in awe of—people who suffer for a cause, who show
great endurance and courage, people who do things which seem impossible—are no different in essence from you or me. Often they will recount
that something took them over. They felt a power which they had never
experienced before, or that their prayers had brought peace in the face
of hardship, which enabled them to survive. Somehow they managed to
reach that spiritual level of consciousness—often unconsciously in the
face of extreme pain or compassion—and that contact opened the door
to a reservoir of spiritual wisdom, love and power.

We do not need to be *in extremis* to be aware of this help. Through the
practice of meditation and service through prayer, we can become mind-
ful and active on more than just the physical level. White Eagle was once
asked if it was possible to remain aware of this higher consciousness all
through the working day. He replied that it is difficult, as we read next;
but then he also gives us pointers as to how to develop this awareness, not
just in meditation, but at times when we are at our most retentive.

It is possible, but difficult. It comes with continual aspiration and
self-discipline. As you progress on the path of continual meditation, you get two levels of consciousness. That is to say, you may
be engaged in everyday things on the surface, but beneath the
surface there is always this consciousness of the universal divine
love. You become aware beneath the daily consciousness all
the time.

Meditate as you go about the world simply by not letting the
'head brain' be always uppermost. Sometimes, in the country,
when walking through the lanes, endeavour to become in tune
with the eternal life behind the manifestation of trees and flowers.
Meditate upon the grandeur and glory of God's universe so that
the 'heart mind' becomes active. Live in such a way that you
are not always thinking of foolish and trivial things; do not fill
the mind of the head with a lot of trash, but let it be usefully
engaged. When you sit at home quietly, let your heart meditate

upon beautiful and joyous and helpful things. How can I best serve others? By understanding them, by helping them, by being kind and thoughtful, by being on the lookout for little ways in which I can be courteous and kindly. This mind in the heart can become active, glorifying God.

Meditate morning and night. Begin with a morning prayer to your Creator that you may be His–Her servant this day. As you go to sleep at night, utter a prayer that you may contact the highest planes of life. This is the most important meditation of all because, as you go to sleep, you are going out into the etheric and spirit world. If, instead of going to bed with your mind cluttered, you can go to sleep with a mind on God and a pure spiritual state of life, then when you are released from your body in sleep, instead of just hovering above your physical body or nearby, clinging to earthly conditions, you will go straight away into the supernal, the Elysian, and there you will be instructed by your teachers in the temple of knowledge and wisdom. When you return to your physical body in the morning, you will feel so happy. You will say, 'Oh, I have had a wonderful night, and I feel so different'. Of course you do: you have been away in the world of light!

We suggest that you prepare yourself the very last thing before falling asleep, even if it is only for two or three minutes. The angels are waiting to guide you towards the temple of wisdom and instruction, and if you go with them you will absorb wisdom into your higher mind. In time it will percolate through into your everyday, ordinary mind.

Developing the senses of the soul

As meditation proceeds, one may become more and more aware of having senses finer and subtler than the earthly ones. These senses correspond to the earthly senses in some ways, but in meditation they can seem also to be one and the same, in that it is possible to smell a taste, or see a feeling. It is not like looking with the outer eyes, for example, but of having a vision which is an extension of thought. White Eagle explains that it is through the development of these senses, even while on earth, through such means as meditation, that we can begin to perceive that life is not limited to what earthly perception shows us. It is said casually that some people have a sixth sense, but White Eagle tells us in a passage from the book, SUN MEN OF THE AMERICAS, that when this sense is truly developed a small part of the true reality—the broad spiritual life which is hidden from most of us—can be touched.

Every pupil who entered the mystery school … began his or her studies by disciplining and purifying the physical body. He or she learnt to eat pure food, and never to inflict suffering upon the animal kingdom. He or she learnt of the vitality and life in the air, and how consciously to breathe in the life-forces of the air. He or she learnt the cleansing property of the element water, not only for the physical body, but also for the psyche.…

He or she learnt how to draw strength from the earth, and how consciously to absorb into the body the lifegiving rays of the Sun. In other words, he or she was taught how to become purified, revivified and sustained by simple attunement to the elements.

As people learnt to use all these elements in their daily lives, their physical bodies became purer, lighter, less weighed down with earth, thus enabling the spirit to come into fuller contact, through the physical body, with other beings, and with the whole great brother–sisterhood of life.

He continues:

The ancient people also grew their food with knowledge and understanding not only of physical, but of spiritual law. They did not stimulate the earth artificially, but grew their food under natural conditions and called down upon the earth the great light—this wonderful element of the Light, which is love—to stimulate life in the earth and 'manure' their vegetation.

All these things were taught under the name of the Great Law; and knowledge and understanding of this Great Law will come back again to people with the development of their soul senses. Even now these truths are beginning to percolate into your consciousness: knowledge, for instance, about the healing and strength which can come to you from herbs and through the finer vibrations of flowers.

This life in the heaven world is open to every soul on earth. No matter how lowly, how ignorant, the individual has access to that golden world of God by its own aspiration and work and service to others on earth. It is important for you to understand this, and to establish the ideal in your heart. Your earth life pulls you down; your brain limits and imprisons you to the five senses. But we remind you that the five senses are only a part of the senses which you have at your disposal. Other senses which will reveal the heaven world to you are, in this time and age, slowly developing in your soul.

In course of time the soul and the spirit will unite and become as one. This is not so at the present time—the spirit is, you might say, 'above' the soul. Rightly, however, the soul is the body of the spirit, and is built from the next ether surrounding physical life. The spirit percolates through the soul, through the senses of the physical body. You have been told that in meditation you can extend these physical senses to the higher ethers. You can absorb the power of your own spirit so that it stimulates the soul senses, enabling them to pass an awareness of higher or heavenly things through to the physical brain. You see with the eyes of the spirit. You see with your spirit and what you see is reflected onto the physical brain. The physical brain is the recipient or reflector of the senses of the spirit, when the spirit is sufficiently developed to impress upon it the finer vibrations of the heaven world.

We want you to understand that every sense has its spiritual counterpart—there is spiritual vision and spiritual taste and spiritual hearing and a spiritual sense of smell and touch. All these senses, when they are fully developed, will bring a sixth sense into operation in people in the new age. It is not easy for us to put into words exactly what this sixth sense is, but we will explain it in the following way. As you learn to disentangle yourself from the heaviness of the earthly life, from the heaviness of the earthly body and the limitation of the earthly mind, you are able to rise in a weightless state, right above the earth plane, and reach the heaven world in full consciousness. This is the state of consciousness attained by the Christed ones through all the ages—a state of consciousness described not only in your Christian scriptures, but in all the scriptures of the world.

Every man and woman has the power within their soul to receive impressions of beauty, impressions of heavenly things from these higher planes; and not only impressions of heavenly things, but also impressions coming from other people and other states of life. God has placed within your own soul a wonderful receiving instrument. By true, deep meditation you touch truth and, at the same time, learn to develop all your finer senses.

Each one of you has the gift of the spirit within your own being, and it is through this spirit that you will learn to overcome death. On your evolutionary path, you will learn that death is only a transition from one level of matter to a higher ether, and that within you is the power to build a bridge: a bridge across which you can travel in full consciousness into those higher spheres and communicate with your loved one. You can see the life he or she is living, and enjoy with him or her the beauties of the heavenly garden. You can taste the heavenly fruit, drink the heavenly wine, and eat the heavenly bread of life. Do not let the material and dark thoughts hold you down. Refuse to be bound. Cut clear of the bondage of the physical world, and rise in sweetness and love into the arms of God.

Cultivating a sense of Oneness

White Eagle has already emphasized the importance of our contact with the natural world, both in meditation and through physical experience. One of the further benefits of contemplating the natural world or, if possible, of spending time in nature (no matter how cultivated), is that it brings a sense of wholeness and Oneness. This awareness is of all life being interconnected, and of the cyclical and therefore eternal life-force which creates and dissolves in a never-ending pattern of light and dark, day and night, seed and harvest. Even at the equator there are seasonal changes to growth, and through these patterns of life nature speaks to us of continuity in the midst of change. The old leaf of autumn is pushed off the branch by the growth of the new Spring bud. Nature speaks to us also of the interdependence of all things. A bird carries the seed of the fruit to new soil, and a whole cycle of growth is born from the new tree. An insect pollinates the flower and the seeds germinate. White Eagle uses images of seed-time and harvest frequently in his teaching about eternal life and the growth of the soul, and asks us to contemplate images of flowers and trees in order to understand who we are and to receive illumination.

The interdependence I see in the natural world brings to me a clearer understanding of how important our being part of the whole is—how crucial our preservation and protection of the natural world—and also brings a deeper feeling, which is hard to describe, of Oneness. It brings a feeling of a life which is not only balanced and creative in every degree, but also whole and healthful. It is hard not to see the hand of God when I walk in the woods in Spring, stand by a stormy sea, look into the perfect heart of a flower, or stand under the immensity of starry space on a clear night. It is also harder to see myself as separate from this magical process of eternal life, which we all tend to do when we are caught up in the affairs of the concrete city and the worldly mind.

The natural world can be our teacher in this sense, but White Eagle assures us that it also brings us closer to the awareness of spiritual union through more subtle means. When we are surrounded by nature, and particularly if we are in the wild places, then the angels and elementals (those inhabitants of the etheric world who are intimately involved in creation) are closer to us. They touch us with their awareness of the oneness of all life, and in that moment we may feel part of everything; we may know that however much we may change, we cannot die.

White Eagle's image for the place we can find within is 'the garden of the spirit'.

According to a person's sensitivity, he or she may receive impressions via the soul or via the etheric body and nervous system, from a state of life which is not exactly outside the physical but it is penetrating the physical life. For instance, if you are attuned to the soul life, you may receive, as you walk amidst the beauties of nature, impressions which will give you vision into the etheric world within the natural world.

Raise your consciousness above the fears and turmoil of the earth, and it is like ascending from a fog into peace and beauty. It is like quitting a wilderness grown barren and ugly and stunted, and following a path into a beautiful garden, fragrant with flowers and the song of birds and running water, beautified by sunlight, by colour of flowers and trees. In such a garden, God speaks to you. God does not speak—at least, God's voice cannot be heard—in the market place. The market place means the material earth. God's voice is heard in the peace and tranquillity of the garden of the spirit.

This garden has grown familiar to us, and probably also to you; but it is not necessarily only in a garden that the voice of

God can be heard. We ourselves have a favourite retreat set by the side of a great blue still lake, surrounded by mountains, often crowned by rose and gold at dawn, or sometimes shrouded in a soft white mist. We often rest here beneath tall and graceful pines, inhaling the freshness and fragrance of the air of heaven. In these conditions we commune with God.

You also need to retire to a similar place within your own consciousness, and then you will become aware of the eternal presence of God. At such times, when you hold inner communion, the voice of truth speaks. You know then that God is wise, you see the grandeur of the Creator's plan, you know that all is working out for good.

So may your daily practice be meditating in the morning on the source of life, the Great White Spirit, and His–Her creation: meditating on the power which lies in the Sun, in water and rain, in the winds and in Mother Earth. You are related to all these elements. They are part of you, you are part of them, and there is that sympathetic chord between you, and in the future you will learn to unfold all these gifts of your soul and your spirit. As a matter of course you will commune with the unseen. They will no longer be unseen, they will be visible, the angels and the nature spirits, and those whom you love who have vacated their physical bodies. They are still there, but at a higher level of consciousness. Don't you see what is going to happen? As human kind unfolds these powers they will be raising the vibrations. As you raise your own vibrations by making yourself more sensitive to life beyond the dark veil of materiality, so you will be raising the whole planet.

When you send out the light to the bereaved and sorrowful, you send out light onto the mental plane to stimulate in humanity the same inner comprehension of life in the cosmos, of life in the spirit spheres. You do not live only on a physical plane, but there is life in surrounding spheres, and vibrations playing upon the earth from your own solar system. You are living in a world of activity on the mental and the spiritual plane. As soon as you learn, within your own soul, to touch the switch which will set in motion those particular rays—cosmic rays and rays of spirit life; rays which are touching your own brain and which are in parts of the brain which are at present dormant—as soon as this opens, you will become alight with the beauty and the power of that spirit world and spirit universes. We want to bring to you a broad and high vision of the real life in which you all live.

You must depart from the idea of separateness. On the physical plane all is working for separation. The mind likes everything cut and dried, everything beautifully labelled; and so the mind likes to think that it was once perhaps Mary Queen of Scots, or Joan of Arc, or some other great name. The mind desires to know *who* it was, to put itself in a little parcel and label it, and say with precision, 'That is what I was. Now isn't this definite and satisfactory?'. Or if perhaps the past life was that of a villain, the mind delights to think, 'I was a bad lot!'. It loves to look at its own picture.

The mind works for separateness. But remember this, the mind is doing its work by guiding humanity towards individualization. Individualization up to a point appears to be separation, isolation. The mind works for the separateness and the individualization of the soul, the ego. That is its rightful function. But as a person evolves and attains a finer individualization, the soul desires identification or unification with the whole, and will lose that sense of separateness—not lose itself, but actually identify itself with the whole. So instead of being an individual, small, compact, isolated, the soul becomes the universal, non-separate from the greatness of the mind of God.

We should like to bring you to recognize non-separation and

help you see that it is necessary to develop towards individualization and growth, but also to develop towards unification and
identification with the whole.However, let us get this quite clear;
our own particular work must be done, but ours is not necessarily
our neighbour's work, nor is our neighbour's work our work. It
is *essential* that we get this unification of thought; this realization
that each path is good, according to the level of consciousness
and the karma of the individual who follows it, but also according to the needs of the general plan for the spiritual evolution
of humanity.

Souls are like drops in the ocean or grains of sand on the sea-
shore. Yet each is individual. Each is a unit, but all blend together,
making one grand whole. Many people fear that when they reach
that high level of spiritual life they will lose their identity in God,
but this is a mistake. God has created you His–Her daughter
or son. God has created you as His–Her child. Of course, you
are a part of God. But you have been given an individual spirit.
So when you unite with all the spirits, with the great family of
God, you are still an individual and retain your own identity.
You will not lose that identity. We would raise you in spirit until
you feel in the great silence and stillness that cosmic life and at-
one-ment. This is the meaning of what your Christian church
calls the atonement. It is the love of the Cosmic Christ raising
all people to that level of at-one-ment. It is the love of Christ *in
you* which causes you to attain a degree of spirituality in which
you comprehend God's love.

We can see this longing in the hearts of men and women for
God. And this is natural when you consider that there is that
desire and that search for a conscious union with the infinite
and eternal Spirit. Because within your own soul is that spark,
that fire, that divine life which is surging upwards—reaching
out to find a home, reaching out to find that link with its source,

so that the perfect circle is completed. We think of the straight line which appears to you to be straight, but actually it is not a straight line, it always inevitably curves round and eventually joins up in that complete circle. And in the centre of that circle is the divine seed.

Now this is very simple. You can put it to the test yourself. You can sit quietly, if you can get that unruly, earthly mind quiet! If you can sit quietly and breathe in the peace of God, you can feel then that you will be raised in consciousness. And you will begin to see form or colour or life at a higher level of vision. And you will *know*; as surely as night follows day, you will know that you have within yourself something which is related to all, not only form of life, colour and sound which is radiating all around you—but around you in all people. If you will sit in peace and quiet in meditation and just try to realize or imagine this life, this life of spirit, life in a higher ether all around you, you will feel that you are part of it. That is the point—you are part of 'IT', you are part of the Whole. We have often said to you 'in love there is no separation'. Of course not, because love is God, and when you love you are with God, and He–She is in all life, all peoples. Never forget this relationship between yourself and the Great Spirit.

PART TWO : FACING DEATH

IV. WHEN LIFE SEEMS
TO BE THREATENED

SOMETHING to keep in the forefront of our minds as we read White Eagle is that, as he often reminds us, he too once trod a path like ours and therefore he understands the fears which we face. The suggestions in the next chapter or two come out of my own experience with patients who have come for spiritual healing, with clients who have come for counselling, and from events in my own life.

One of the hardest things that can happen to a person is to be told they have a life-threatening illness, such as some form of cancer. Shock is indeed the word which one uses to describe the initial feeling for many people because, no matter what they suspect, there is still the moment of impact when the mind immediately plays the worst-case scenario. It can then become numb, or go into overdrive to try and find a way out.

People react to shock and fear in a variety of ways, but chief among the responses are panic, anger and powerlessness. Indeed, the anger often stems from a feeling of powerlessness. It is the way the body, or what White Eagle would call the 'body self', knows to mobilize energy to do something. For those people with a faith, or who are following a spiritual path, there can be added the feeling of guilt: both for becoming ill in the first place, and then for having negative feelings about this.

What is more, the mind begins to worry on behalf of relations and friends, especially children. It tends to project feelings of loss onto all the things which will no longer be seen or done. It asks again and again the question, 'Why me?'. Above all, the person may feel intensely vulnerable and helpless. No matter how hard the mind, now being used to help, tries not to allow these feelings to surface, they arise. The body self—that is, the mind, body and feelings connected with the earthly self—will naturally feel threatened, even if only occasionally, and without any regard for the individual's beliefs. For most people, dealing with feelings and thoughts about what is happening to them will become part of a constant struggle as time goes on.

All these thoughts and feelings (though natural to the body self) do not help the bodily system at a time when it needs extra support. They produce added tension, however much they may be the mind's way of trying to come to terms with what is happening and mustering some sort of defence. It is not easy to go against the body, and to do so would set up more unwanted tension. The best way forward therefore is not to fight these feelings but to channel them usefully. This is the way White Eagle would advise to those who are seeking to train the body self to deal with life in a more spiritual and holy (White Eagle means by this a 'wholistic' or 'healthy') way.

The positive response to hearing negative information about one's health requires a balance of energies, as most things in life do! On the one hand, it is important to be pro-active and regain a sense of being in control; on the other, one needs to relax and trust in the goodness of whatever plan unfolds for this part of one's life.

One of the first ways to do this is to use the energy from the worry and anger to find out as much information as possible about what is happening. Then the right decisions can be made; the patient (and their carers) can prepare for eventualities and come to terms with the process. This will have the benefit of the patient feeling more empowered. To counteract the feeling of powerlessness, it is necessary for them to take charge of their life, and not let others do so, which is the natural tendency.

However pro-active we need to be, it is equally important to relax. White Eagle reminds us often about this. Relaxation needs to take place as often as we can remember to do it. There has been much research in recent years into the benefits of relaxation on the immune system. At times of imbalance in our bodies the immune system is understandably under greater stress than usual, and so anything we can do to support it by relaxation is helpful. The secret is to give the body self the opposite message from the one brought about by fear, and that is that all is, in fact, well! The earthly mind may deny this, and so may the body if it is feeling sick or in pain, but there is another part of the mind which knows this fact very well indeed, and which can be used.

To help with this, some sort of regular daily practice of centering ourselves by attunement, prayer or meditation, some time when we consciously align ourselves with the higher mind, will be invaluable. It is important to be regular with this, even when it is a tough choice, or when we are surrounded by the bustle of hospital procedures. It will enhance the feeling of doing something positive. At the same time, we can help by attuning to a trusting place within, where the very cells can get the message of wellness and thus the support they need. White Eagle stresses the importance of asking for help from the calm spirit; asking for help to relax and trust. People are often astounded by the sense of wholeness and peace which comes from being able to relax and trust in whatever is.

Relaxation is harder to achieve when there are all sorts of strong emotions underneath the surface, and so another way of relaxing is through releasing strong emotions in a safe and supported way. Often doctors and hospitals will have trained counsellors they can recommend, who will know how to help a person to offload feelings of pain, guilt, fear and frustration. They are trained to support the person when they cry and rage, in a way which family and friends might find difficult and frightening. Consciously letting these feelings happen is not running contrary to what spiritual teachers say about controlling these emotions. In fact, it can be a way of regaining control of feelings which have been thrown into chaos. Through counselling, one can find a balanced way of releasing tension and difficult emotions in a totally supportive environment.

Relaxation

What follow are White Eagle's constructive and salutary words about our need for relaxation, many of which were given to patients who had come for spiritual healing. I find it helpful to remember again that he has faced all these circumstances himself at one time or another.

We would say one or two words about relaxation. You are all tense, and it is for your good and your health and your peace of mind to consciously practise relaxation. Test yourselves, and you will be amazed to discover how tense you are. Endeavour to get the feeling that the world is holding you up instead of you holding the world up, and you will be surprised how much easier you feel. You cannot hold the world up, God does that. And God upholds you. Whether you believe it or not, it is true. God is running your life, God is upholding you, if you let Him–Her. Try to adjust yourselves to the Almighty Power, the Almighty Presence.

You feel you have too much to do; but, you know, it is not the amount of work, it is the way you do it that causes you to be battered and worn out; it is your attitude of mind towards that work. If you are interested, and put the God in you into whatever you are doing at that moment; if you do one thing at a time quietly, and do not have a million other things in your mind at the same time, then you will find that you will get through all the work you have to do quite calmly. At the end of the day you will feel refreshed instead of worn out and like a piece of frayed string.

Don't try to make things go the way you want them to go, but centre your whole aspiration upon the light, and the realization of the power of the light in your own heart. God's plan is wiser than yours. Trust in God.

Relax, be still. There is nothing to fear. Let yourself float in the ocean of the Infinite Love. Be still and know God....

Just rest; feel that you are sustained on a great ocean of strength and of unending peace. Your needs are all known to the hosts of invisible and angelic presences, and every true need will be supplied. Have confidence in the Source of your life. Be still; all is well.

Non-resistance as a powerful healing tool

When things happen to us which we do not like, then it is very likely that we will have a resistance to them. We have a resistance to pain, a resistance to difficult circumstances. That resistance can produce a great deal of anxiety, and where there is anxiety there is often tension. Where there is tension, there is more pain.

This resistance is something which Buddhists tend to call 'aversion'. Buddhists have developed various meditation practices where one does not turn away from the things in oneself and around oneself that provoke aversion. One just sits with them. The point is not to resist anything, or run away from it (our usual reaction to pain) but simply to let it be. This practice may break the self-generating cycle of resistance, tension, more pain; and it can be a very powerful tool. White Eagle talks about the same process many times in his teaching. He stresses Jesus' teaching about not resisting evil,* and he often talks about acceptance.

When we are resisting what is in the moment and trying to escape it, then we can also miss solutions. In addition, we can miss the real spiritual help which can come from within, because we are not seeing what is 'here' any more. Solutions arise out of really focusing, rather than avoiding, by relaxing into each moment that is. We may not like the conditions very much, but if we relax into them—no matter how painful, awkward, difficult, or embarrassing they may be—we prevent a cycle of resistance which can produce worse effects. Perhaps it was to help prevent that cycle of resistance and its negative effects that White Eagle talked about relaxation to healing patients.

Living with the moment—no matter what—is extremely powerful; and far more powerful than wanting things to be different. If we really believe that our spirit is in charge and that whatever is happening at this moment is absolutely right for us, then it is right. White Eagle says that in each moment you are creating your future, so in each moment must exist both the creations of the past and the seeds of the future. By keeping ourselves centred in the now, we can find the way out of the process and move into

*Mt 5 : 39

the future only as it comes. Perhaps even more importantly, we can trust ourselves while it is all going on, even when things look grim.

When we are resisting, it is usually because we are afraid in some way. The opposite of fear is trust and faith. The spirit is in everything, even in the most painful things; even in the pain itself. There is a holiness in our total involvement in each moment, because when we are present, God is there in the moment with us. Seeing God, we can trust the absolute rightness of the moment, and relax into it. No matter what is going on, there is great release of tension. A feeling of peace comes, even when things are at their most difficult.

It might be very hard to believe in this peace being possible if you are already in pain when you read this. Every part of the self at such a time understandably wants to escape, not to surrender. It is worth attempting, however, if it means a release from the cycle of tension and the opening-up of possibilities for healing and change.

Perhaps you would like to try an exercise, either at the present moment, or some other time.

AN EXERCISE IN 'LETTING GO'

Whatever difficulties you may have at this moment, seek to relax. Wherever you are, and no matter what is around you, sink into a state in this moment, and the next and the next, where you can feel that every single part of what this moment offers you is right. With each out-breath, feel the tension in the physical body pouring out, like sand out of a sandbag, and take a few moments to breathe in trust—imagine it is like a sweet and gentle perfume which flows into every cell and softens all resistance.

Think of this moment, in all its complexity, as being right, presenting you with exactly what you need for the next moment, and the next, and the next. Feel all the muscles in your body responding to this message, which is a benediction of trust, as if every part was receiving a comforting massage. You may find yourself saying inwardly, 'I am safe. All is well'. There may be parts of you that will deny this. You need not fight them, but simply keep letting the sand pour out of the bag, and let the moment be.

Rest assured. All is well.

Fear of death

White Eagle says that to help people overcome fear of death was, and still is, one of his primary tasks, for fear is a feeling which may come and go in us frequently. Therefore, in the next passages, we take a look at fear generally, but particularly the fear of death, and ways in which we can deal with this strong body-self reaction in order to come to a place of deepest healing within ourselves. There is a hymn by J. G. Whittier, some lines of which read: 'And death seems but a covered way, Which opens into light'. When this is sung I find I can almost hear a silent prayer, 'Dear Lord, let it be so!', issuing forth. There are certainly many documented accounts of near-death experiences, where the person attests that they travelled along just such a covered way into the light.

It must be heart-rending, once one has passed through the veil of death, to touch the consciousness of humanity and to feel how afraid many people are. No wonder that many of those in spirit, including White Eagle, remind us so frequently and clearly that we need have no fear, and that death is part of a beautiful journey to a place we know as home.

However, it is hard for those who are afraid to be reassured by words. Fear creates mistrust, and therefore anyone wrapped up in a cloud of fear may find it difficult to trust evidence of a life after death, or to own that death is not the terrible experience it can sometimes seem. All evidence can seem suspect, one way or another, and the only recourse many people who are in a state of fear can find is to try to put thoughts that could actually sustain them out of mind.

One of the troubles with fear is that it is inhibiting and can be all-consuming. It is also insidious, in that a fear in one area of life can influence other areas. This is certainly true of fear of death. It is sensible not to do things which put the physical body into grave danger, but when fear rules the mind, one can become so imprisoned and restricted by what 'could happen', that life is limited and not lived to the full. Many things which are joyful have an element of risk attached to them, and life can become joyless when we are constantly inhibited by a 'what if' thought in our minds. Conversely, facing up to a fear of any kind brings confidence in all areas of the self, and a very welcome sense of release. What we were afraid of may shrink into true proportion—or even cease to be an object of fear altogether. Trust takes over again. It may begin with trust in oneself, and then extend outwards. If you trust yourself, then you are able to trust yourself in relationship to life and to others. Trust in others develops. With a trust in life comes a trust in God.

One of the best ways to face our fears, as White Eagle says, is in the presence of wisdom and love, through a creative process of meditation. If we can contact an intelligence and understanding that is beyond our fear it can enable us to develop a little detachment from fear's often all-consuming nature. White Eagle reminds us in a beautiful passage in THE SOURCE OF ALL OUR STRENGTH, 'It is natural for you all to fear the unknown, but you can be quite sure that God is in the unknown'.

The inner being which we contact in meditation symbolizes, or reminds us of, a part of our self which is outside the weight of our fear, and yet intimately aware of our best needs. This is the part of the self which White Eagle is constantly asking us to find, not only because it lifts us spiritually, but because in making contact with that level of being we find a place in ourselves where fear is not. It is a place which is beyond and above the fear, yet still part of us. That place is one which can become more and more real to us. One day we will exist there fully, rather than in the fear. Through a process such as this we may get a flash of awareness of a reality beyond death, or catch a glimpse of where we wish to be—and can be. It sounds simple, but this initial step of listening to oneself, and being listened to, is profoundly creative and may bring about a change in our whole consciousness.

There is an exercise overleaf which shows how meditation can be used as a way of dealing with fear. You may discover, as you go through the exercise, that your fear is a fear of loss or of change. Coming to recognize and accept the positive outcomes of change can help to overcome the fear of loss which death seems to bring. You may, for instance, remember times in the past when a feared event actually did come to pass, and yet be able to recognize that the change which resulted has produced growth, awareness, new experiences and gains. Loss may be what was experienced at the time, yet now the experience seems positive, one which has been creative of good. The sense of loss, in other words, was temporary, and the real loss not irrevocable, as it once seemed it would be.

In the passages which follow the exercise, White Eagle sought to comfort those who were afraid, and to speak to the heart of those who felt keenly the loss of a friend or loved one.

A MEDITATION TO HELP WITH FEAR

Find a place to sit quietly, where you will not be disturbed, and where your spine can be straight and your eyes closed. Begin with the practice of God-breathing. White Eagle describes how effective this can be.

'As you breathe deeply', he says, 'you are affecting the mental and astral bodies. All the higher bodies are affected thereby. Keep the spine straight because the forces travel up the centre of the body. As you inhale each breath aspire to God. Feel that God is entering into you. As you exhale bless all life. Do not breathe in a strained way: all breathing must be harmonious and offer no discomfort. Breathe slowly, quietly, harmoniously.'

If you are breathing in the way White Eagle describes—harmoniously , and with awareness of the spiritual life-force flowing into you and from you—then you will begin to feel more calm and still inside. You may experience a feeling of real poise.

When you feel ready and at peace inside, imagine yourself in a sanctuary which you create on the inner planes. It can be exactly as you like. but somewhere where you feel comfortable and uplifted. Imagine here a focal point of light and power. There is a feeling of deep love and peace, and you may see a being of light who is your guide and friend for this process.

Ask for help, and then tell this person what most frightens you about dying and death; what the worst thing is that you feel could happen. They listen with complete love and understanding, and with no judgment of your fear.

Explain, also, how that fear affects your life. Allow yourself to feel comforted by the simple fact of being listened to lovingly as you face your fear.

When you come back to the outer world, do something which is affirming of yourself and your life—something which is creative, and nurturing, whether it be walking, working in the garden, making a cake, writing a poem, or simply writing down the experience you had in meditation.

Have you ever thought that you are a part of God, that you are a thought of God? Meditate upon this and you will probably be overwhelmed with the greatness of the idea. You are a thought of God and you are held in the mind of God. God has created the universe. God has given you eyes to observe that universe; has given you a brain to understand; and has given you a heart to love. He–She has given you hands to serve and help life and your brother and sister, and feet and legs with which to walk. He–She has created you a perfect human being with wonderful powers to live, to learn, to see, to enjoy and to glorify His–Her creation. What a wonderful gift is your life!

You live not only for a few short years in a physical body; your life has always been and always will be. It goes on and on and on; it has no beginning (although we have said that the soul was breathed forth from the Father–Mother). It has always been in the Infinite Life and always will be. When your individual life was breathed forth, you were sent on a journey. People say: 'What is the use of it all?'. We answer that the gift of individual consciousness, of self-consciousness and, in time, God-consciousness, is a beautiful and wondrous thing because to live (although you do not realize it) is glorious and beautiful. Having been breathed forth, there is an in-breathing again, but you do not lose your life; instead there is change from one state to another. Each stage of the spiritual life or the spiritual journey unfolds more beauty.

If you are worried today, careworn, anxious and fearful, we would beg you to stop and think. Look back over your present incarnation. Review the troubles and trials that you have passed through, not forgetting the joys and the happiness also. Remember again past trials, anxieties and sorrows. Then see how you were brought through them. God has never left you without help, has never left you alone. Always, events have come along which have improved your conditions. Even if you cannot admit that your material conditions have improved, there has surely been a development in your spiritual state? You have learnt lessons which have brought ease of mind. You are wiser. Through your difficulties and trials light has entered into you. In other words, your consciousness of a divine love and a guiding hand has grown as the result of past events. It is therefore a mistake to fear the future, which can bring an ever-increasing consciousness of God, an ever-increasing understanding of God and God's life. It is a mistake to fear death. There is no death.

Beloved children of earth, we know that in most hearts there is grave fear about what lies on the other side of death, the side you do not see; and our desire in giving this message is to bring to you consolation and comfort. Most people know only the physical aspect of death. They watch a friend in what appears to be the agony of death, but which is far more often a quiet, peaceful passing away of the consciousness. That is all, a passing away of the *consciousness* from the physical body. But it leaves desolation in the heart of the onlooker, a great fear. 'Oh, if only we had faith to believe that all is well!'—that those who pass onward will not suffer, or be unhappy, when separated from us. 'Surely, because of their devotion to us as well as our devotion to them, there may be sorrow and loneliness on their part as well as ours at the breaking of the physical link?'. It is to bring you consolation and perhaps a deeper understanding that we speak on this subject.

You may imagine that the soul who passes on will feel lonely. We remind you, however, that there are guardian angels and friends of former lives, even ones you may not know, waiting to meet the soul. So there is no question of lack of companionship. There is very happy companionship waiting for most souls in the spirit world.

What we say will, we hope, make you understand that there is no separation at death. By this we mean that when a soul passes on to the next state, which is usually the astral world, it finds itself in exactly the same state of life as the one it goes to every night. When you are what is called 'asleep', you are living for a time in the astral world, and there you are meeting former companions of your earthly life. It is all a matter of harmony; and you are drawn to those with whom you are in harmony. So for the one who passes, there is not the separation you imagine, because at sleep all meet on that sphere of reunion. Your sleeping here is like the waking over there on the astral plane. So you must dismiss all thought of separation when the change called death comes. We repeat, there is no separation. There is no death. It is just a continuation of conscious life.

It is perfectly understandable that we should place our sense of security in the things and people about us. I believe it is also true to say, however, that our quality of life and happiness is based not only on what we have or do not have, but on how we think about what we have, or do not have! It also depends on how we respond to and make use of what we have. For example, a rich, beautiful, intelligent, creative person can be as bored, unhappy, hurting, lacking in confidence and afraid as anyone else. A person lacking many luxuries in life may feel quite content with their lot. Happiness is a sense of wellbeing, and does not exist in us because of the things, people, attributes or events which are in our lives. Rather, it is there because of what we think about life. Sometimes we think wellbeing will only come if we are materially provided for, if our relations and friends are in good form, if we are healthy and fit, if we are busy and creative, if we have a loving partner, if others seem to like us, or if we are slim or strong or young. In this case, we are often going to be unhappy because we will be afraid of never finding these things, or of losing them once we have found them.

By contrast, recognizing how much our fear is based on projections into the future that have been based, quite unfairly, on past experience, can give us a determination to live in the moment. If we do this, it may not matter whether we have the things we want; we may even find we can let them go altogether. This is the opposite of denial through blind pleasure-seeking (our fearful self's attempt to hide from fear). A conscious acceptance of the joy to be found in every moment, no matter how limited our life seems to be, is a key to releasing fear.

No-one, I think, is more aware than White Eagle of how difficult it can be for us to accept what lies in each moment. There is a counsel of perfection behind what he says, but despite the difficulty of putting these thoughts into practice, our encouragement is the knowledge that ordinary people have tried to do this, sometimes in extreme conditions, and found immense relief and a new joy in life. We cannot always do it, by any means. There are days when life is really hard; there are weeks when we do not remember, and times when we feel so strongly about something that we cannot think of anything other than our sense of loss or fear. All we can expect of ourselves is that we will eventually come back to what the heart tells us is true, and that one day all the pain and fear will be dissolved in understanding and peace. White Eagle once said: 'For every seeming loss, a rose is grown in the soul garden'.

Being here and now

Other than through constant self-examination, how does one avoid the attitudes which turn into fear thoughts? White Eagle's advice is, 'Centre your whole thought in God and learn that fear's bondage over you will tomorrow pass away, and you will behold the light'.We shall shortly look at the whole passage from which this is taken.

The more that we can keep in the back of our minds (or just beneath the surface, everyday thoughts) an awareness of spiritual things and of God, the more that deeper understanding will positively influence us every moment. We can learn how to do this through our daily practice, whether in meditation or prayer, and also through thankfulness for every moment. This is 'practising the presence of God'. The divine presence will drive out all fear; it will make itself known to us; and it will respond to our sincere prayers for help in times of need. White Eagle never tires of telling us that the handle of the door to the heaven world is on our side. What that means is that it is we who have to create a channel by which the Great Spirit can reach us. Fear blocks up that channel, while our deliberate focus on God reopens it.

Fear can also lead to depression, partly because the emotion of fear feels overwhelming and the object of fear seems unalterable. However, a positive response to fear cuts through the layer of hopelessness, and allows a shaft of creative, healing light to reach us from the source. 'Do not despair', White Eagle seems to tell us, no matter how often the feeling of fear arises: 'Keep on opening the door. Thus you allow a shaft of creative, healing light to reach us from the source'. Centering yourself in the way White Eagle describes at the beginning of this section is a method of taking charge of your life. His reassuring statements always uplift, and point the way through that hopelessness towards peace.

Do you fear death? But why? Death is a very beautiful experience. The masses concentrate on the sordid aspects, but to the soul pressing forward, death is a glorious experience.

Never fear death. No amount of worry will extend your life. There is nothing to fear. There is no death. There is only a laying aside of the coat of skin, the physical body in which you have descended into matter, to the earth plane. You have descended in search of knowledge and wisdom, and in search of experiences to enable you to function from the Christ within without the limitations of the finite mind. The experiences that you go through are those which enable you to function in the infinite spiritual realm. This is the whole purpose of life.

Whatever your trouble of mind, brother or sister, concentrate—that is, centre—your whole thought in God and learn that fear's bondage over you will tomorrow pass away, and you will behold the light.

Joan's Story

Years ago, actually in 1952, I had to go into hospital for a serious thyroid operation. It went well, but at about 9.00 pm my throat felt very tight and uncomfortable. About two hours later I suddenly felt blood running all over my chest. I was given oxygen, and the matron phoned the surgeon who had operated on me. He was doing an emergency operation on someone in another hospital, and asked them to send me by ambulance to him. As I was being lifted into the ambulance, the matron checked my pulse and I heard her say, 'She is too weak to be moved; she will be dead before she gets to the hospital'.

Then I seemed to be floating down a long dark passage. I was aware of my aunt, who had been a sister in a Dundee hospital, with me, and also of a man in Quaker clothes. There was no pain, and it was as if I was separated from my body, but still aware of being connected to it. My last thought before becoming unconscious was, 'Is death like this?'. I learned later that my husband was sent for, as I was not expected to live.

I came to soon after, hearing the surgeon saying, 'It's a miracle, she's completely conscious!'. This experience changed my life.

In 1999 my younger son was taken ill with cancer. He died suddenly of a heart attack, and three days after he died, when I was sitting quietly on my own at supper time, I sensed his presence beside me, and then felt his hand placed over mine. He always used to do this, if I was upset at any time, a silent love which told me he understood how I was feeling. He said, 'Tell everybody that I am all right'. Then there was a great wave of love, and he was gone. At his funeral I saw him standing beside his wife with his arm around her. Although I felt a great heartache at the loss of his physical presence, I know that death is not the end, and that we live on in another world of a different vibration or wavelength, 'closer than breathing, nearer than hands and feet'. It is a blessing to have this knowledge, and to have experienced its reality.

V. FAITH

THERE ARE those who go on seeking for conviction, because the hunger of love urges them to find out where some loved one goes at death. But one can obtain proof of the continuity of life after death. Never mind if the seeker only contacts the immediate next world … the lower astral plane. All serves a purpose, and is true; and it is right that communication and proofs should be given to the enquirer. But the deeper students of the mystery schools know that life is continuous. If you know, then the light is born within; you leave behind the search for evidence, which is but an endless repetition—like a gramophone record ever repeating the same thing. The light within says, 'I *know*; there is no death; my loved one cannot die; he, she, still lives'.

Becoming aware of God at every juncture, so that fear passes away, is also seeking to live in the moment. Fears are often the result of thinking hopelessly into the future. Engaging fully with each moment of life leaves no room for fear. As White Eagle has reminded us, the earthly mind often engages us in a self-perpetuating cycle of worry. To absorb the mind in the very process of life and in what is going on around us right now, gives it an involvement which is positive and hopeful.

Hope is helpful, but perhaps it is even better to have faith. Hope is future-orientated, but having faith is present-centred. That is to say, we may have faith that whatever we choose to experience physically will be the best for our body. We may have faith that whatever is happening is right for us. We may have faith that the healing can work through the surgeon's hands, or faith in the drugs prescribed, that they will be good for us. When we do this, we are telling the body something positive about what is happening now. As White Eagle says, 'Of a certainty, as you think, so you become. So you become physically, so your character is developed, so your surroundings are created'. The body hears thoughts, and if the body hears positive things then it will relax. Then the body's own resist-ance will not inhibit the process of healing.

So it helps to have faith in all that is decided. It helps to trust our deci-sions. It helps to have faith in everyday life. It helps to have faith in the body. The disease we suffer may be the body's way of trying to cope with some area of tension in the life, one which has got out of hand. It may be, in fact, a positive attempt on the body's part to self-heal. The body needs praise and support, not condemnation and fear. Thus we may help it to change its present response to stress.

With faith, every moment is an opportunity for change and love and healing. Thus one may see how hope is dependent on the projected im-age of things changing for what one sees as the better, and always has a touch of fear in it: 'Oh dear, I hope so'. By contrast, faith is concerned with what is happening now, and there is no disappointment, because all is as it should be. Yet what is happening now is not immutable; there are always possibilities for change!

White Eagle has always encouraged us to have this kind of vision of eternal life—not one which is dependent on wishful thinking, but one which is based on the rightness of each moment. A useful passage on this is to be found in his book FIRST STEPS ON A SPIRITUAL PATH (originally entitled MORNING LIGHT).

Never think that you are alone in your difficulties. We have in mind those of you who are 'up against it' at this moment, not knowing where to go or what to do. You are blindfolded, but only temporarily. Contain yourself in confidence and peace, longing only to be God's servant, praying that you may be still, and await His–Her commands. All is known to God and the agents of God.

For while no soul is left in isolation, every soul must pass through its initiation alone. Every soul must also pass from one state of life to another alone. It is this very aloneness, this mist which shrouds the future, which eventually forces the soul to progress. At first the soul is like a child in thinking itself sufficient, believing itself able to accomplish anything and everything, capable of solving on its own the puzzle of living. Yet it is through the resulting loneliness that it discovers the true Source of its strength. Indeed, on occasion that soul will specially need to be alone; for when the long-blinded eyes at last open and the soul's expansion or quickening takes place, it must be in solitude. This may happen to you: perhaps in this period of bondage you are purposely being left to yourself in order to develop your inner strength and faith in God.

What is this faith? Faith is an inner knowing that God can never fail in goodness and love. Every soul must develop this faith in God; not only this inner knowing that God is good, but also faith in the God within itself. Encased as you are in materialism, you are very easily misguided. It is as if a descending shutter had blacked out your awareness of the spiritual life about you. That is why earthly matters seem to you far more important than heavenly. Your real self is battened down in the hold of your own ship of life. That ship is your soul, which is being tossed hither and thither on the seas of emotion until in your extremity you cry out to awaken the Master of the ship, the Christ. On the instant, he arises and says, 'Peace; be still!'. The turbulent emotions subside and all is peace.

A few more words of White Eagle's put this in the context of what he calls 'initiation'.

You become aware then of a great calm within, and a voice says: Lo, I am with you alway. You know this is true. Not only do you hear the voice of the Master, or our own voice speaking, but an inner voice is also saying: 'I am the Lord Thy God. Within, my child, within is your strength, is the power, is the divine will'. Nothing can happen in your outer physical life that matters more than this, your own initiation into the expansion of the God-consciousness that is yours.

All is as it should be

Every life is most accurately and perfectly planned according to the vibrations which the soul has built into it in the past. There is the most perfect organization. Although there are millions and millions of souls incarnate at present, with every one of these children of God there is the perfect working out of the divine plan and pattern.

As we have pointed out, with each incarnation the soul has a new brain, and the memory of its past lies not in this brain, but in vibrations in the soul accumulated over many, many lives. Memory of the past rests with a man or woman's ability to become aware of these. When he or she does become aware, the past begins to reveal itself, and he or she can then feel certain soul-desires urging certain courses of action. He or she now begins to realize the reason behind these desires and urges. In meditation, remember, you must turn from the outer world, the world of action, to the inner world. In such periods of quiet a man or woman gains increased understanding. He or she may begin to realize why there are specific urges or feelings within. They may perhaps indicate that there have been previous lives as a soldier, a king, a minister or priest, a sailor or a teacher. Moreover, he or she will find these memories actually working themselves out in the present incarnation.

I believe that White Eagle is trying to tell us to have faith that at every point in our life we have been seeking the light. Sometimes this has been in a defensive way, but nevertheless, he says, we do have an innate urge to grow. Positive thinking such as this will have a profound effect on the body's cells and on the healing process. It also helps us to live in the moment, and to have faith in every moment of our lives. It can provide the courage to face our fears, and to feel, even in the midst of crisis, that all is well. In one of his prayers, White Eagle helps us 'to be strong to accept the experience which comes to us, knowing that it comes as an opportunity to expand and purify our vision. May we be true to our higher self, which has asked for light'.

White Eagle was once asked this question: 'Would it be correct to say that it is impossible for anyone to make a major mistake—to take the wrong turning, to choose the wrong path?'. This was his answer.

That is a wide question, one which needs careful answering. In a major event affecting the whole incarnation, the soul cannot make a mistake. A deep intuition will urge the soul to take a certain path, and even if it appears to be wrong to all onlookers, the soul unconsciously knows that it has to tread that path, for karma is directing the soul. It is in the little things that more play is given. Sometimes trifling events—a careless word, the missing of a train, the picking up of a book, will change a whole life. You will say, 'If it had not been for this trivial thing, the whole course of my life would have been different!'. But the trivial thing has happened. The angels and the lords of karma have been watching closely. God, says your Bible, *shall give his angels charge over thee ... lest thou dash thy foot against a stone.* No being has any power to upset the divine plan—God does not allow the universe to slip out of His–Her hands like that. There could not be anything outside the will of our Father–Mother God.

So many of you are frustrated in your daily life because things will not go the way you want them to go, and you become very

disillusioned with the teaching about God's love. But we would assure you that as you daily strive to overcome all doubts about the
love and wisdom of God, you will be getting nearer and nearer
to an expansion of consciousness. In an expansion of your own
consciousness you will feel, and be blessed, with heavenly joy and
comfort and assurance that in God's world all is well. And what
about this world? Is all well for you in this world, on the physical
planes? Yes, my dears, it is. It is you who are sometimes out of
step, not life. You want things to be different from how they are,
when what the true aspirant is after is complete acceptance of
the wisdom of God's laws.

Sometimes you can make contact with your loved ones who
have passed into the next state of life. Those dear friends of yours
are living in a world of sunlight, an intensely beautiful earthly
state. If you could draw aside the heavy curtain of materiality,
you would look into a world of perfection, into a sunlit life of
harmony, softness, where there can be activity and also passivity
when the soul desires passivity or rest. Then there are spheres
beyond the astral, spheres of great activity where beings who
have passed through all grades of the lower life have now found
freedom; where they can study the heavens, if they so desire, or
can study music or art, literature or sculpture. Any great longing
of the soul is there given expression. Such spheres are infinitely
more beautiful than anything you can conceive while you are
imprisoned in your box of flesh.

Remember, although you are imprisoned in it, your box is
similar to the casing of a radio. You have knobs you can turn,
and you can tune into other realms. You have also been given
wings but have not unfolded them yet. Why do you think that
the Egyptian Pharaohs were called 'winged' Pharaohs? They had
to learn to use their wings and rise above their limitations. You
are also learning to do this today, but you have only just com-

menced the process. You get disheartened and allow yourself to be overcome by the heaviness of matter.

How can you break through the darkness which envelops you? Only by developing the divine will in your heart, the will to obey the law of the Christ life. And how are you going to develop this will? Well, we will tell you of a very simple measure—so simple that you may take little notice of what we say. Every day and all day seek to obey God's command to *love the Lord Thy God with all thy heart, and with all thy soul, and with all thy mind;* and *thy neighbour as thyself.* 'Thy neighbour as thyself': this is a very subtle command. It does not say *more* than yourself, but your neighbour as yourself. Love the Lord Thy God with all thy heart and with all thy soul and with all thy mind, and thy neighbour. That is all. That is the law. But it is not simple.

If you are going to obey the law you have to do it physically, mentally, emotionally, spiritually. This means you have got to command your thoughts. You have to bring the divine will into operation. You have to will the will of God, not only for yourself but for all life, so that you recognize the Omnipotence governing the world and also governing your own life. You may have an idea that such and such a happening would be just right for you, but in a year's time you may see how wrong it would have been. You can look back upon your life and know that had you had your own way things would have been very different. You have to admit that there is this gentle, guiding hand which is so wise. Had you gone your own way entirely you would never have learned some of the great truths, nor would you have attained any measure of inner peace and spiritual joy.

It is your reactions to the events of daily life, not the events themselves, which are important … the happenings in your life should be regarded as tools placed in your hand to fashion and shape the material of your soul. There is a small arc of a circle in which the human soul vibrates or can swing, and a man or woman can choose within this arc. The choice is given to him or her in order that he or she may gain experience. Outside that arc the soul has no power. It may look as though you have made your own choice. But recognize, behind all, the divine guidance. Although it appears accidental when certain things happen, we can assure you that the divinity within directs life. You are guided and directed by this wonderful law. Therefore, never think that you could have averted or changed things in your life. The Great Architect of the universe holds the plan, all is working together for good. The divine purpose declares that as you react so may you receive greater strength, greater light, greater truth. In that sense you have freewill. Your reaction to outer circumstances is the thing that matters.

Humanity has to have a choice, but that choice is to learn discretion; to learn how to discern truth…. Every time you respond to a good, to a higher, to a spiritual impulse, you are helped by your guardian angel. That pure light from heaven can help you to be kind, tolerant, patient and faithful, and all the qualities that the soul needs to grow; but it must be by your own decision, your own freewill. On the spiritual path much is expected in the way of self-discipline, but no-one is bound on the spiritual path; it is a difficult path, but only a person's own freewill holds him or her to it. You are not forced to walk the path—you are at liberty to return to the world and live a worldly life. But that part of your spirit which is indwelling in matter, because of the soul's past experience and the wisdom it has gained in previous incarnations, knows that if you choose the path, then it can only follow the light. Knowledge of such a path is your joy and consolation in life. It also brings with it soul gifts which enable you to penetrate the enveloping mists, the confusion and the darkness of physical life.

This is the way you reach ultimate freedom. As the soul progresses through incarnation after incarnation, the more it responds to the urge to love, the sooner it arrives at its destination. This is freedom—and yet, at the same time, unification and at-one-ment with the Christ light. The soul does not lose its individuality through following the path of love; rather it grows and expands in power, glory and beauty, and its individuality is increased and expands. In your reaching, eventually, the state of freedom yet at-one-ment, simple human kindness to each other is of the utmost importance. This means that the vibration of kindness is built into the structure of the soul. In its next incarnation your soul will possess an impetus to be more and more kind and to bless the world with the spirit of tolerance and love. Simple kindness is the secret of the freedom towards which your soul is working—freedom from continual rebirth, freedom to rise into the light and to become at-one with the Christ heart, the Christ light. Love, my brethren, is the way to eternal life and eternal freedom. Love is the way to all knowledge, to all understanding.

Looking death in the face—Robert

Having worked as a relaxation therapist in the HIV/Aids field for the last decade, I have on many occasions been in the privileged position of supporting people who have been preparing for their transition to the spirit world. There have been times when the person has been so close to passing that their aura was one of unearthliness, such was its brilliance. Often I would sit with someone and their eyes, glowing, deep and so clear, would feel as if they were looking right into me. Many people might have found it an unnerving experience, but to me it was a most bonding time—spirit to spirit.

One occasion that stands out in my mind was when I was treating a client whose friend Tom was 'dying' on the residential unit upstairs from

94

where we were. Although he was in a near-death state, his passing was not imminent. He could have gone on for another few days, so the doctor attending to him said. Halfway through the session, with my client relaxed on the cushions and myself in a semi-altered state (it usually happens this way, for some reason), I saw for a fleeting moment the solid form of Tom in the residential unit. He looked radiant. He then smiled, looked at my 'rested' client and then disappeared. I remember thinking that maybe he had just popped out of his body to see what was going on elsewhere, or that I had been thinking about him previously and he was on my mind.

After the session I mentioned this to my client (who has since passed on himself) and we proceeded to go upstairs to the residential unit. When we got there we were informed by one of the nurses that Tom had 'died' about half an hour previously—around the time he had appeared to me in my consulting room. Clearly he wanted to say goodbye to his friend. I sometimes wonder what their 'new' lives are like and maybe one day I will meet with them again, just to say 'hello'.

Faith is based on trust

Although faith can be independent of any proof or experience, it seems to me that it does require a degree of trust. This trust has to be, first of all, trust in our own perceptions and beliefs. Through this trust in ourselves comes trust in others and in life itself. When we trust life, then we can begin to trust what happens in each moment, no matter what it is. Trust is a quality necessary to a responsive life—to wellbeing. Trust helps us relax, be creative, respond to what we see now, and be spontaneous. For me, this trust in life and living is one of the initial and vital steps towards developing faith in God and in eternal life.

However, to trust is not easy, and what is more, trust can often be broken. What inhibits complete trust for many people is that life does not seem to be fair or consistent, that there seem to be dangers in many areas of life, and that death awaits us at the end. These thoughts can underpin our lives. We may be able to forget them for a while, but many of the things which we do in reaction and defensiveness or to compensate ourselves are based on a lack of trust, and the fear that follows. These are the kinds of preoccupations which White Eagle addresses in his teaching.

Often a lack of trust in a situation or person, when analysed, reveals a lack of trust in oneself. Given that we cannot change the behaviour of others, and often cannot change the circumstances of our lives a great deal, then what we need to do is to begin to learn how to trust our self and our own responses to our life, and to those people we encounter. We need this self-belief even more when faced with an illness, or difficult life-choices.

It may sound strange to say so, but to find this trust in a situation is, I believe, often the first step towards having faith in God. When you trust yourself, you trust that inner awareness that comes in meditation, for example. When walking in the beauty of nature, you trust the voice which speaks in your heart and says: 'I know there is a divine plan'. Without that trust in your self, you are always doubting the subtle, inner things you experience, as well as the more mundane ones.

In most cases, as babies we entered this world in complete trust of our selves. As a small child we did not question how good, lovely or wise we were, nor what we saw or needed. It is only as their lives unfold that people begin to lose this trust. How to reconnect with it is one of our challenges, and perhaps one of the major purposes of our life, for in doing so we begin to find that in trusting the earthly self we become aware of something beyond it, which is the indwelling spirit. White Eagle now takes up an earlier theme, of self-consciousness as a vital first step on the way to God-consciousness.

Yes, there is indeed a divine plan of evolution for all creatures. Indwelling in all matter is a supreme creative power that you call Spirit, or God; matter lies, shall we say, unconscious of the divine power which brought it into being. The purpose of the descent of the divine spark into matter is that it may develop a separate consciousness which slowly evolves through all forms of matter, until at last when the soul reaches a certain level of *self*-consciousness, it becomes aware of a divine life buried deep within. This life is like a most beautiful jewel, a transcendently lovely gift secreted in man–woman.

Remember that the sole purpose of your life is to grow first of all in self-consciousness—that is, consciousness of yourself as an individual. Then you expand your consciousness to take in those around you, those with whom you live. Shall we call this a family consciousness, a group consciousness, consciousness of the whole brotherhood of life? You have sometimes expressed in meditation the intense joy felt in this realization of spiritual brotherhood—which of course is the true spiritual communion. The joy accompanies that development of the soul towards awareness and the needs of those around it. In the same degree as the individual progresses, so collectively the whole race approaches this point of brotherhood and awareness. Then will come an expansion still further towards God-consciousness or cosmic consciousness; and then the next step is the consciousness of the Solar Logos, the solar consciousness.

The whole purpose of incarnation, the purpose of life, is for the soul to develop this self-consciousness which later broadens out into God-consciousness. The development of self-consciousness is, shall we say, the beginning of individuality. The ego has become clothed in flesh. It has become, shall we say, God incarnate! But this beautiful truth is not recognized, is not apprehended in the early or unconscious stages. The child, the babe, from its birth gradually develops awareness of its surroundings, gradually develops self-consciousness. What you perceive in the unfoldment of the child, so you will also recognize in the spiritual evolution of the adult. In its crudest stage, the soul is struggling for self-expression and to attain self-consciousness because it has come from the Whole, from the divine Spirit. It is a spark, an out-breathing, an offshoot, a seed of the Godhead. And it remains unaware of itself or its potentialities. The whole work of the soul from the beginning is to develop itself. You see this going on everywhere. You see the effort made by the soul to gain this consciousness of itself. For this reason a great deal of selfishness comes about, because the soul is innately selfish.* Its very work is to find self-expression and self-consciousness. This process long endures until later the soul begins to be aware of something other than self (that is, the part of the soul concerned only with its own development). The soul becomes aware of a spark within, which is the God-spark, the flame. At that event the unfoldment of God-consciousness commences. In this process the soul learns the necessity for making silent the outermost plane upon which it is living. This accomplished, it will have to attain silence on the emotional plane and then on the mental until it becomes aware of the place of Silence. There only it finds its true self; it accepts its relationship with God.

This development from self-consciousness to God-conscious-ness takes place through a medium—not a medium in the Spir-itualistic sense, but a form in which the soul can express itself. The form of expression of the individuality through its many incarnations is simply the human personality. The development of the individuality takes place over many incarnations, and it results from the development of the *self-conscious* state. And the personality comes from the development of the *God-conscious* state in a man or woman, and is its expression. We will illustrate this by drawing attention to the personality of the avatars, the Christs. Among them, the personality of Jesus Christ is the greatest example. But both the Lord Buddha and Jesus Christ expressed the individualized soul. Buddha, the beautiful, gentle, wise, still personality through whom the golden light just *shone*, came from the heart of the Omnipresent, the Omnipotent and the Omniscient. Jesus developed the personality through whom

For an explanation of the use of this word, see p. 168.

the sweetness and beauty of the light of Christ manifested, so that men and women could understand the meaning and the power of divine love. In the life of Buddha there was a pointing of the way, a revealing of the path which the soul must tread on its upward climb towards its Father–Mother God. That way was the renunciation of desire.

Some may ask, how did the teaching of Buddha on desire-lessness harmonize with the teaching of Jesus the Christ? Was it right that the soul should attain this degree of desirelessness and seek Nirvana, the place or state of consciousness that is sometimes interpreted as arising out of the annihilation of the individuality?

We reply that if people believe that the attainment of Nirvana is the annihilation of individuality, then they are wrong. There is *never* annihilation of individuality, but instead an at-one-ment. This stage is called Nirvana because the soul reaches a condition of utter love, peace and at-one-ment with universal life (though it does not remain in that state for ever more, by the way). At that moment, the soul comes into the fullest understanding of the meaning of the three Principles which underlie all life—Love, Wisdom and Power. When the individual soul enters at-one-ment in a sense it loses itself, in that it goes into the ocean of God-consciousness. But it *always* retains its individuality. Therefore, the reason for the descent of the soul into matter is that it may receive full experience of matter and so grow in individuality and in God-consciousness that in the end it holds mastery over physical life.

Why do you fear to fall when you know you can fly?

When compiling a book I find that I often get inspiration by strange means. The intuition works overtime, and 'they', the spirit brethren, have all sorts of ways of making me take notice! The same was true as I worked on this book.

One morning at the beginning of my meditation time, and after I had been up and about for half an hour, I remembered that during the night I had dreamt of flying. I have had many dreams of flying, and they are always very special for me, so I was surprised to have forgotten this one. The dream involved many different flying experiences, but I remembered one in particular where I was sitting drawing on top of a very, very tall wall of a roofless castle or old monastery—one leg crossed in front of me on the wall, the other hanging in space. I had flown up there to paint a picture, and had become absorbed in the scene in front of me, when suddenly I looked down at the drop beneath and became afraid of falling. I sat there with the adrenaline of fear coursing through me for some time, until I suddenly realized—remembered—that I had flown up on to the wall.

Why should I fear a fall when I knew I could fly? I remembered thinking that one reason was fear of the unexpected: the fall would not be deliberate, unlike taking off into the air when I chose to fly. In many ways, my fear was of the sudden panicky feeling I might have as I realized I was falling, rather than of what would happen. What does White Eagle say, but that the greatest fear is fear itself?

What is life but a time when we have forgotten that we know how to fly? So often our fear of death comes from forgetting who we really are, and the inability to find ways of remembering. When we attend a service of worship, go into communion, or are led in meditation, then we are enabled, perhaps, to touch a part of ourselves which does remember that we are greater than the earthly self, and therefore survive its death. But another way in which meditation and worship can help us with our fear is to change our focus of attention from the fear of death to the longing for union, for Oneness. When longing for God fills the consciousness, then the transition of death becomes a very minor part of the completion of the circle. When eventually we do have to 'fall', we will rediscover the joy of flying free into another reality. We shall soar into heaven on wings of light.

Links between heaven and earth—Marion

My sister died at the time of the twelve-noon sending out of the Light. A lovely day, windows wide open and a gentle breeze which carried her spirit quietly away. I saw it leave her body, a white pearly mist which rose from the bed and slowly moved to the window and disappeared. There was just the softest of *sighs* as it happened, the loveliest sound I have ever heard and the loveliest sight I have ever seen. Even now, after twenty-two years, I can rest in and find a peace in the experience. It was a reality which will never leave me.

My mother, before she died, told me of a beautiful white butterfly which played about the room. I suggested the wings were angels' wings, but she insisted it was a butterfly. When her ashes were scattered on my father's grave we stood a while in silence. A white butterfly settled on the grave and stayed for a few minutes. It was a most poignant send-off.

A question of timing—Colum

This is a very personal story, and although Joan, my aunt, was a very special and widely-loved person, it is at the intimate level that this story works, for so many others could tell their own and very different story about the same events. Joan was diagnosed with Acute Myeloid Leukaemia some eighteen months before her death, and she had plenty of time to make herself ready for the moment when it came. Of course there were low moments, but her radiance throughout all this time is what we all remember, and how perfectly she handled all this period of her going out of this life. The length of time for which she survived was considerable longer than is usual for this disease, and the medical care she was given was only supportive—there was no chemotherapy, no radiotherapy. So her end was, above all, very 'natural' in its timing.

In the autumn that it came, I was away in Scotland for periods of several days at a time. I knew, when I went, that I took a risk each time; but I had her blessing, and believed I only needed to be ready to fly south at any time.

When the call you are expecting comes, it is always in another sense unexpected, though. British Airways were excellent in getting me onto the very next flight without any extra charge, and my friend drove me to the airport in Inverness; but otherwise I had the most frustrating of journeys, including an hour-and-a-half's extra wait at the airport. Only a refreshing drive home through the night air helped me recover my spirits.

Yet my timing could in no way have been improved upon. I hit, to the minute, upon Joan's last really lucid spell, even though it was 10.30 at night when I hurried into her cottage. It was as though she knew exactly when I was coming, although no-one else knew the time. Indeed, she had apparently said earlier, 'I will wait and see Col, and then I will go home'.

Everyone left us. We had an absolutely wonderful, and deeply intimate, conversation in which she most beautifully wished me well in my life. It was as though, in no way that she had ever done while fit and well, she had looked right into, and addressed, my innermost soul.

The following afternoon the summons came to be around the bedside. Quietness, a long wait, a slowly-filling room. Figures either side of her, stretching out to reach her across the width of bed, gave the tableau a feeling of including angels by William Blake. My mother sat erect, meditative: with her, I am sure, more at the inner than outer level. I realised that just as Joan had wanted to see the fulfilment of my dream, so in a sense this was her own dream come true. To die with her family all around her, united: 'all one' as she would say.

Later—these words are from my notes at the time—I believe I saw her slowly edge herself out, like a little child in a white gown; one moment half free, then three-quarters free, seven-eighths free, and so on until finally just the toes of each foot held. Then she seemed to be standing tiptoe upon a rail, flexing the feet up and down, like a diver on a board waiting to dive, waiting for the precise psychological moment.

I realized next that I could make better contact with her spirit by being in the garden outside for a bit, and came back in later. When she passed, it was almost imperceptible, but I am quite sure that the very second of it was pre-chosen.

VI. SUFFERING

A NUMBER of White Eagle's teachings were given before and during the Second World War to groups of people who were almost certainly afraid, angry and appalled at what was happening in their world. Many were at home, confused and bereaved, and others were away with the Armed Forces. Grace Cooke herself, White Eagle's medium, had never been a stranger to bereavement, and the headquarters of the Lodge in London were destroyed by bombs. It was into this climate of uncertainty and horror that White Eagle brought much of his quiet teaching about such subjects as karma and suffering. He, and those in spirit for whom he speaks, knew what people were going through then, as now, and the concerns which were uppermost in their minds.

First and foremost for those on any spiritual path was the question which so many ask today: 'How can a loving God allow such suffering to occur, and to innocent people?'. I was writing and compiling this book during and after the events of September 11th, 2001, in the United States, and during the subsequent war in Afghanistan, when such questions were clamouring for answers in people's minds once more. Such dramatic events shock the world, and bring insecurity and fear to the forefront of our consciousness; they can make us question the nature of our existence, and the existence of a loving Spirit.

We are extremely restricted in our vision while on earth. We identify strongly, and rightly so, with the limited physical form in which our consciousness resides for a time. We do not truly 'see' what happens at the moment of death, neither do we 'see' the soul and spirit of a being who chooses its moment of passing, or understand how this can be. We have no knowledge of the motives of the spirit, nor the spiritual yearnings of the soul, which may cause it to take on what seems to an outsider to be extreme and appalling karma. We do not know the far history of a soul, or group of souls. It is helpful to remember that each one of us is infinitely more than the earthly personality.

Those brethren in spirit who speak through White Eagle and use him to bring their message to the earth remind us of this blinkered vision in order to help us get beyond what we perceive with our physical senses. Indeed, this is what all spiritual teachers do. They seek to expand our perception beyond the physical life, to prompt our imagination to conceive something else happening, even at a moment of extreme horror. They try to expand our awareness of what life is *really* all about. They tell us it is not about the pleasures of the body-self; it is not about storing up 'treasure on earth'. Life is not about earthly happiness in the restricted sense in which we know it; but it is about spiritual joy, and the eventual spiritualization of all matter so that death is overcome completely. They remind us that, as both a soul and spirit, each of us knows this, and so we sometimes choose pain and hardship while on earth, in order to grow through them and develop this spiritual understanding and joy.

Those in Spirit remind us that we choose pain in order to serve a greater purpose. We make this choice, they say, not only for ourselves, but for humanity and the world as a whole, since part of spiritual understanding is the knowledge that all life is one. Therefore we sometimes choose to experience shocking things in order to help awaken others. We serve others through our suffering and 'death' by forcibly bringing imbalances to humanity's collective awareness. We may, individually and as a group, choose to die through starvation, through persecution, through war, through murder, and to do it in such a way that the world cannot ignore it, but has to take stock. Possibly the whole of humanity is ready for a major initiation—a significant heart-opening. If so, it will be a vital move towards bringing spiritual 'brotherhood' closer into manifestation on earth. This does not justify the violent acts of others, but it does explain how all is used, ultimately, for good.

In the passages overleaf, White Eagle shares the breadth of his vision to present another possible reason for sudden transition, and helps us understand more about the karma of suffering and the eventual overcoming of disease and crucifixion.

Life on earth is governed by a just, loving and wise law called the law of karma. What you are now, you have to a very large extent created for yourself, having caused yourself to be placed in the conditions in which you now find yourself. Appreciation of this fact should not lead some people to be proud and others despondent, but rather bring a sense of tranquillity and loving acceptance of all things they are called upon to do and to bear.

We say this because many of you have been disturbed by disasters. You have wondered why innocent souls should suffer. In the first place, remember how limited is your vision. You only see half the picture. You do not see what would have happened to those people had they remained in their body in the particular conditions and environment in which they found themselves. You think that a God of love would have left them exactly as they were to pursue their way. Remember that God uses His–Her Lords of Karma and even lesser beings who have it in their power to bring about certain conditions for the good—always for the good of the man or woman. If you see disaster, do not wring your hands and say, 'How terrible! How could God permit such a thing?'. The wise man and woman immediately says, 'God be praised, for God is all-wise and all-loving. And God without doubt is saving His–Her child from some catastrophe which would be indeed unhealthy for their soul and much worse than this'. For this reason always look for the good in any happening. We know of many, many instances where souls, men and women, have been gathered into loving arms in the world of spirit. We know of a loving care which has seen the conditions confronting that soul and has said, 'This soul has had enough. Come home, my child'. Remember that you cannot know what is on the other side of the material curtain.

We ask you to accept what we say. What we describe is the spiritual law, and you can learn to accept such happenings (which are hard to understand) as the result of the working out of a law. Sometimes people suffer and are very sad. Their lives appear to be broken up and in a state of darkness; but it is not lasting. The condition passes, and the sufferer gradually undergoes a process of spiritual expansion. With this comes a light, a joy and a beauty unknown to the vast numbers of people who do not have the experience. Yes, life grows beautiful when you search for the beauty of God in every incident right through life.

Growing in harmony and understanding

On the subject of suffering, White Eagle was once asked whether disease could eventually be overcome, and this is what he said.

Most certainly. Goodwill is light, and each man or woman learns to create a body of light which interpenetrates the physical atoms. When the physical atoms are permeated with light they become light and are raised above the normal vibrations, so that they cannot be seen by physical sight. Jesus was visible to his disciples and then he disappeared. The atoms can be so raised in vibration that they are seen at the ordinary human level, but the substance of the body was not the same dense substance as in 'dead' men and women.

In time that will come to the human race. Then the physical body will not die of disease. Disease is due to lack of harmony. A master can leave the body when he or she likes and assume it again at will. The physical body is a dress, a vehicle, but it can be composed of higher, more purified atoms. Alive means alight.

Within you are the two aspects of life, positive and negative, wisdom and ignorance, light and darkness, spirit and the pull of the body, the pull of earthiness.... Your true purpose is to develop the son of God within your soul. We understand the conflict which ever rages in the hearts of men and women. We do not blame. We do not condemn. We see instead a process of spiritual unfoldment taking place.

Up to the time the disease takes over, what you might call its crucifixion, the soul undergoes many temptations and tests in the wilderness; it is tried on the physical, emotional, and on the earth plane. Even you yourself will recognize certain soul-experiences through which you have passed in this life as being minor crucifixions. Through these you ask yourself: can I learn to use the mind, not on the lower level, but on the higher aspect, and can I hold fast to the Christ standards?

Love is ever attending your soul in the form of a guide, in a human form, as well as an angelic guardian. Once you cry out earnestly for help, that help is already there. We would have you know also, that the crucifixion only affects the lower nature, which is worldly. This is the nature whose values are of the earth; the nature that clings to material things which will crumble to dust and ashes. The only everlasting and real life is that of the Christ within, and that life is not crucified. Christ is not crucified, but freed, and rises triumphant into the heaven world.

It is often hard to understand the reason for suffering, even when we know there must be one. White Eagle was asked this as well: 'Sometimes when a soul is suffering, it cannot always discover the reason. Is this really so, and why should it be?'. And he replied as follows.

No, even if it recognizes that it is learning something, it is paving the way for its own greater understanding. The truth it seeks will come in a flash, perhaps some time after the suffering has passed.

You are learning the lesson of patience, and also the lesson of love and constancy. When you have to go through difficulties, hold fast to the love of good. Never mind what happens; if you are blinded and unable to see the reasons for suffering, keep the light burning in your breast, saying again and again, 'God is my Father–Mother; God is all good. God will bring me safely through'. Do not cling to material things or even to people. If they go, let them go. If they hurt and disappoint you, that is to teach you. There is only one thing to fear, and that is fear itself. Strive to overcome fear, fear of death, fear of life, fear of loss, fear of suffering. This is the goal—to overcome all fear, and to realize that you are a child of the Father–Mother God. You are moving forward rapidly to the great awakening. You will see a reunion of nations and the people, and a disintegration of the forces of destruction which have been loosed. Look forward, look forward, look forward, not only with hope, but with conviction, to the coming of the brother–sisterhood of humans and of all creation on earth.

When someone you love is suffering

One of the hardest things we have to experience in life is witnessing a loved one, a friend or family member, suffering in some way. When we ourselves are going through a painful time there can come a fortitude, a certain spiritual power, that carries us through; but watching another person suffer, we may feel quite powerless. We may be utterly confused as to how best to help them. As time goes on, especially if the illness is classed by the doctors as 'terminal' or incurable, other difficult feelings can arise, which may add to our sense of helplessness. We long to help, but often we don't know how to do so, or we try to help in some way—only to find, despite our best efforts, that it doesn't seem to work.

Our earthly anxiety, fear and unhappiness tend to get in the way on these occasions. Even though we may know how counterproductive these feelings can be, it is hard to stop giving way to them when we feel powerless either to help, or to make things better. White Eagle tells us that one of the very best things we can offer at distressing times is simply to think positively about the person who is in pain.

These positive thoughts will work on the inner level to strengthen our loved one, to bring him or her encouragement and support. Our positive attitude of mind will open the door to the power, wisdom and love of the spirit, which can then guide our actions. One way White Eagle helps us is by suggesting the use of affirmations. Affirmations are positive statements, directed to our deepest selves. They can contradict the automatic, negative, earthly responses we sometimes have. These positive statements can change our thoughts and our feelings about what is happening.

It is generally easier, because of the pull of earth, to think in negative terms about what happens than to spot the truth behind any situation. The positive awareness is harder to grasp, especially when we are observing someone obviously struggling with pain or fear. Positive affirmations remind us of the spiritual truth behind life and of the mercy, wisdom and love of the spiritual plan. Positive thought reconnects us with something greater than the suffering. Sometimes it can give a glimpse of what is profoundly noble about our loved one as they go through the suffering.

In the pages which follow is a set of affirmations based on White Eagle's wisdom, put into the kind of language you might use when thinking of a friend or family member who is suffering. It is important to realize that they are not suggestions about what to say to someone, but thoughts which you could hold in your heart to help you both. Through the repetition of these positive affirmations in your heart, you are helping yourself to remain positive and trusting, and to have faith in the effectiveness of your support; you may find your relationship with the sufferer is improved, and, since people do pick up on your thoughts, the patient may be helped to feel better about themselves and what is happening to them.

There are three columns. The first is what you are trying to avoid doing by making this particular affirmation. The second is the affirmation itself, and the third contains a suggestion of the positive effects each of these affirming inward statements is likely to have on your loved one.

Also, and perhaps more importantly, the statements are all generated to affirm the power of the other person's own spirit, as well as the wisdom of God, and therefore to create a broad, clear channel for that inner spiritual strength to reach through to sustain and support them.

AFFIRMATIONS TO USE WHEN YOU ARE
HELPING SOMEONE WHO IS SUFFERING

WHAT TO AVOID	WHAT TO SAY TO ONESELF	WHAT THIS MAY ACHIEVE
...exacerbating their fear.	'I have faith in your ability to get through this.'	You are believing in them at a time when they may doubt themselves—you give them hope.
...being patronizing.	'I respect your path even when it is different from my own, and therefore I will not assume I can see what you should be doing.'	They will feel your respect and be encouraged. They will not feel patronized, but truly supported.
...increasing any feelings of isolation.	'I know that you may need to unburden yourself from time to time, and to release your feelings, and I am here to listen. You will have my love and attention in which to hear your own thoughts aloud.'	You are helping the person to release their difficult feelings, without them feeling alone or weak when they do.
...the tendency to offer advice which, though well-meaning, may increase feelings of weakness, and being out of control.	'When you ask for my advice I know you are seeking reassurance that you can find your own way, and that you have the inner strength and wisdom to do so. Even when I am tempted to give advice I will instead encourage and support you in finding your own understanding, and using your own intuition.'	You are affirming their own wisdom, even when they feel helpless, and believing in their own contact with their spirit within. You are affirming that the spirit exists in them, at a time when they may doubt themselves and any form of spiritual aid.

WHAT TO AVOID	WHAT TO SAY TO ONESELF	WHAT THIS MAY ACHIEVE
...increasing a sense of shame and guilt.	'I know that when you feel vulnerable you may say and do things which are not what you really mean to do. I sometimes find this hard, of course, but I will try to understand.'	You are bringing them relief from shame, and your deepest love, at a time when controlling negative emotions is much harder.
...increasing their despair.	'Your karma is your own. I know that the best gift and help I can give is to have faith in you and your continuing essential self; to listen to you with an open heart, receptive to how you feel and what is true for you.'	You are believing in their spirit and their earthly self being one—you give them faith to persevere.
...limiting them through your own fear.	'I know that tomorrow, or even in an hour, you may feel differently. I will think of you as a being with an infinite capacity for change and development, which is occurring all the time.'	You help them to know, by your confidence in them, that no pain is permanent, and that they grow ever closer to love and wellbeing. You give them hope and faith for the future, and increase conviction that changes, even miracles, can be just around the corner.
...exacerbating the pull of association with earthly conditions to the extent that it is difficult to see anything else.	'I know you are spirit. Your spirit has brought you to this place where you are now for a reason. Beyond your physical body I will see you as a shining spirit, and as a soul which is learning valuable lessons.'	You are affirming their spirit, and soul-learning. This will bring confidence in God's plan for their life.

WHAT TO AVOID	WHAT TO SAY TO ONESELF	WHAT THIS MAY ACHIEVE
...the extremes of false heartiness and depression.	'I believe that precisely when life seems at its darkest, you are closest to God. I respect you for going through this period of great growth. I will therefore stay positive for you without minimizing your pain. I will listen to your pain whenever you want to share how it is.'	You will be helping them to believe in the essential goodness of life, and of themselves, at a time when they may be feeling guilty and self-punishing about their reactions. You are also letting them know that you do not think they are morally weak for not being perfect yet!
...increasing lack of self-esteem and a sense of failure.	'I really believe you to be doing the very best you can, and that you always have done so. I will try to help you know this. But I will listen to all your feelings.'	You are helping them to forgive any sense of failure which may be blocking the healing process, or the acceptance of transition.
...increasing anxiety, and feelings being out of control	'I know it helps you to be in control of things as much as possible, and I will therefore try to let you tell me what you need, rather than assuming that I know, and try in my anxiety not to fuss.'	You are helping them have as much control as possible for as long as possible, so that they are confident that ultimately their spirit is in charge. You help them feel respectful of themselves, and so utilize all their strength. You help them not to give in out of helplessness; you help them to have courage.
...increasing a sense of helplessness.	'Although things have changed for you, I shall see you as strong.'	You are contradicting their feelings of helplessness, allowing them to be in need of support without feeling overwhelmed and useless.

WHAT TO AVOID	WHAT TO SAY TO ONESELF	WHAT THIS MAY ACHIEVE
...being critical, and thus adding to their shame.	'When you behave defensively, maybe in anger, or with intellectualism or pride, I will endeavour to see this as an attempt to be in control when your life may feel to be out of control. I will help you in such ways as you allow me to.'	You are telling them they are lovable and worthy of love, at a time when they may be feeling un-lovely.
...increasing feelings of abnormality and isolation.	'I will be myself and act as naturally as I can in your presence, especially when it comes to humour and hugs.'	You are helping them have faith that even this time of difficulty is in the plan; to feel secure through maintaining the safety of normality.
...promoting a feeling of being pitied.	'When I say I would love to see you, then you can be sure that is the truth. I will make sure I only do what I want to do, so that what you get from me is my sincerity.'	You are helping them to feel that you really want to be with them still, and contradicting their feelings of unloveable-ness, unworthiness, or ugliness. You are letting them know they can depend on you.
...exacerbating feelings of being useless—of life being over.	'I believe that you are still giving as much as life as you always have, whatever you feel able to do physically or mentally. I will still ask your advice and ask for your support when I need to.'	You are reassuring them that they are still a worthwhile human being, and that being ill, or suffering, does not mean they are useless, or unworthy of respect. You are helping them believe in the loveliness of their unique being, irrespective of what they can do.

WHAT TO AVOID	WHAT TO SAY TO ONESELF	WHAT THIS MAY ACHIEVE
...increasing a sense of victimization.	'In every way I see you as a whole and responsible person. Just that, at this time, you may need extra support, love, appreciation, encouragement and approval.'	You are helping them feel whole, and that all is well on a deeper level than perhaps they can perceive at the moment, and you are affirming your support.
...increasing their guilt and yours.	'I may not always be able to love and support you in the most positive ways. Sometimes my limited self may get in the way. When this happens I will forgive myself, because it does not make me an unloving person.'	It will not help your loved one or the one for whom you are caring if you cannot forgive your own lapses. They may already feel guilty for putting you through this. They will benefit from your own positive self-regard.

These thoughts are all expressions of our love, ways in which we can inwardly support our loved ones, and encourage our own endeavours to help them wisely. The statements are those which seek to maintain the person's dignity, freewill and self-respect, essential qualities of being human which tend to be threatened by suffering and illness.

Finally, White Eagle helps us to understand how important our feelings are when we are saddened by the suffering of others. He says: 'Remember the importance of feeling, because through feeling you develop the Christ within. As you feel the pain and suffering of your fellow creatures, you are developing the Christ within. Do not be ashamed of your feelings. They are the pointers, the guides which direct you along the path of light'. He then continues to reassure us about some of the feelings we may have, especially when we have been hoping that spiritual healing would produce a complete or miracle cure.

Some people become disillusioned about spiritual healing, maybe because their friend, in spite of all the effort of the healers, leaves them, leaves the physical body. And why should people leave the physical body by means of the death of that body? The soul, at the present time, has not reached that level of complete mastery over the physical body at which it can pass death by. But Jesus taught his disciples, and is teaching you, that there is a way, a pathway you can follow, which will eventually give you command over the physical atoms, so that death as it is known now will not be the same.

Remember, also, that the inner soul of a man or woman knows the day and the hour when it has to leave the physical body. This may be unconscious, but the time of passing cannot be altered by a man or woman, only by the law of God.

We mean by this that however much you try to heal a patient, it may not be the divine will for that patient to be healed, and that patient will know in its own soul when the day of its release from the imprisonment of the flesh has come. When this happens, try to send it forth with your love and blessing into that larger life, that happier life, that freer life. But if, on the other hand, the karma of that patient has given it this opportunity of complete recovery and healing, then that patient will—indeed must—be healed.

So, if the patient passes on, do not make the mistake of thinking that the healing power is of no avail. If the dense physical body is not healed because the karma of the individual does not permit it, nonetheless the soul body, or the etheric body, is still undoubtedly, unquestionably healed, and carried through those limiting lower astral spheres right onward into the glorious, heavenly world of peace and beauty and love.

David's story—by his mother, Anne

David had visited India twice during the two years preceding his illness,

so the dysentery which affected him during and after his holidays con-
cealed the more serious problem. By the time his cancer was diagnosed
he was terminally ill, and his wife—whom we love and with whom he
lived and also shared a business—had felt unable to continue with the
marriage. So, in the space of a week, David had lost his wife and his
home, his health and his job, at the age of thirty-seven.

He came to live with us, his parents, and we gave him contact healing,
as did a dear friend who kindly visited; and we asked for absent healing
from the White Eagle Lodge.

We knew that if he were to be healed we were asking for a miracle,
and at first it seemed that might be possible. We were supported by the
prayers of friends from the White Eagle Lodge, Buddhists, Roman Catho-
lics, Quakers, Christian Scientists, Anglicans, Jews and others and we
helped ourselves by taking the Bach Flower Remedies. While he was well
enough David arranged a new career and study programme in case the
miracle happened, and he attended a psychologically-based course called
Turning Point, which helped him to clear away any limiting thoughts or
resentments from the past.

He practised daily meditation, which became so deep and so important
to him that he often waited until we were in bed and the world outside
had become still. He was aware as a result of these meditations of why he
had the cancer, and grew in wisdom and strength of spirit, which helped
us, his wife and all his many friends. We feel it was his finest hour.

The visiting nurse helped us with various aids and advice on drugs
which kept him very alert and fairly comfortable, and he chose to have no
chemotherapy or radiotherapy. Thus he only had the cancer to contend
with. The doctor said that he had managed his illness admirably. Having him here at home all the time was a great privilege; there was time
to say all that we wished to say and he felt that we had gone far beyond
the parent–son relationship. His life had not been easy and many checks
and disappointments had blocked his path, which was hard for one with
his lively and enthusiastic temperament.

Until three weeks before he passed he was still wondering if the situation would change, and when one day he said to me, 'What do you

think, Mum?', I had to give an honest answer and say, 'Well, it doesn't look like it'. From then on he prepared himself, and found comfort in the thought that he did not have to struggle on through the difficulties which had so often beset him. It meant much to him that we had helped him into the world and were going to help him as he went out of it, and he told his friends that the nine months he spent with us then were some of the happiest days of his life.

Only once did his courage falter, and we helped him by talking quietly and reading him Teddy Dent's lovely poem, 'The Lake of Peace'.*

On the morning of his passing he had been out of bed for a short while, very weakened in body but absolutely alert mentally, and composed. We made him comfortable while we had lunch, after which my husband heard his breathing change and suggested that his brother and I should come upstairs. As we came into the room he opened his eyes and turned his head, and held out his hand to me, saying, 'Come and help me over, Mum.' I answered, 'Are you ready to go?', and he said, 'Oh, yes'.

So we stayed with him and I sat by him with his hand on my arm, and we talked a little about those who would greet him. In my heart I asked Minesta (Grace Cooke, White Eagle's medium) to help him over as she had helped my mother in a similar way, and David asked me to talk to him about Minesta. I then led him into meditation based on 'The Lake of Peace', floating in a small boat along the pathway of light across the water, into the heart of the Sun.

He passed so gently that it was imperceptible, and we felt that we had been with him all the way that afternoon.

David appeared just thirty hours later to a dear friend who had not heard that he had passed, who was giving healing to a patient in his sanctuary early in the morning. David stood quite still, we were told, then nodded to our friend and spoke the words which I was saying to him as he passed, 'All is well'.

The comfort we have gained from the beautiful teachings of White Eagle both during and after this time has helped us immeasurably, and

*This is printed at the end of the book (p. 217) as it may be of use to others facing the moment of death.

the wonderful support of the prayers and healing from our friends at the White Eagle Lodge turned what might have been purely a time of suffering and sadness into a time also of revelation. For this we give our deepest love and thanks.

Courage

To my mind, the previous account is a profound example of courage by people facing life *in extremis*. White Eagle talks about courage in the following passages:

Never grieve for the dead. Never grieve for the living. There are no dead. But what you call death is an initiation, a quickening of the sensitivity of the soul, so that when it is released from the physical body it is able to understand and see some of the glory which awaits it in that higher world, the Infinite and Eternal Garden of the spirit.

We are thinking now of a certain group, a certain brotherhood which you know by the name of the Albigenses or Cathars, who suffered great persecution for their beliefs. But it was worth it because they unfolded themselves to receive this light, and it poured down into them from that world of light. And it gave them power, power to comfort those who suffered, power to comfort the bereaved, power to heal the sick, power to face any ordeal which they had to go through.

Men and women are creatures of courage. If they have received or found this glorious light of the Son or universal Christ Love, they are untouched by persecution by ignorant people.

You look back over history and you see the persecution in your Christian tradition; and you say, 'How horrible, what a terrible thing'. This Light of the Son of God brings to those who are persecuted a strength, a power, which enables them to face any ordeal which they are called upon to face.

Take this to your heart, take it to heart and remember that whatever your problem—whether you are sick, whether you face the great initiation of death, or whether you face poverty, whether you face seeing your loved one suffer—whatever your need, we beg you to know that there will come into your heart a courage and hope, and a vision which will enable you to understand the reason why you are facing such an ordeal. There is no separation when a person realizes that he or she is part of the infinite Spirit, and can say, 'The heavenly Father–Mother and I are one'.

The Brotherhood of the Albigenses in France had received this profound secret of life eternal. They faced torture, they faced death with shining faces because they knew that they could not die, nor could their spirits be imprisoned in a cave or any material prison. These holy brethren (and as we say this there are many such groups all over the world, even to this very day, though they live secretly and quietly beyond the noise and babble of the market place), these quiet and holy beings live their lives in service according to their knowledge, in service to their brothers and sisters of the earth life. They do not fear death, there is no death. They know that the spirit rises free from the tomb of physical matter.

This is the truth which human kind has to learn, and the sooner all of humanity learns it, the sooner there will come a better state of life on your earth.

No-one knowing these profound and eternal truths can live to him- or herself alone. He or she knows, *knows*, and is part of all other life. Such a one knows that everyone is part of the Great White Spirit, and that if anyone inflicts suffering on other creatures or other beings, that person is inflicting it on him- or herself.

This we would emphasize to you, and commend it to you all: the importance and the beauty of courage, which is implanted in you by your Creator. It is not all souls who have developed within them strength of courage, but it is a quality of the soul which must be developed.

Those of you who are engaged in service to humanity may find the path very difficult and find your heart failing sometimes, through lack of courage. We would say to you, 'Look up, dear brethren, look up to the source of all courage. Be not weary in spirit, and be not wearied by what you see on the surface in the outer world. Many of you have touched the heights and heard the voice of the spirit, and you may, at times, be cast down when you contrast what you know is truth, the life of the spirit, with the worldly world. To you particularly we say, 'Look up and pray for courage, and you will not be disappointed; for as you pray for courage, so those who are commissioned by the Great Spirit to help you will be able to draw very close, and bring to you that very special gift'.

Courage, of course, is the ideal; but what if a person passes on to the next level of life in great fear? What if their courage deserts them, or the events of their passing are so sudden, so full of pain, or so shocking that they cannot find any strength within them to face death with 'shining faces'? What happens to them?

I should like to relate a far memory of my own. Through certain evidential experiences in my life, and through meditation, I feel certain that I can remember my life and death as a Cathar. I believe I was a *par-fait*—one of the initiates of the order—and walled up, along with others, in a cave in the mountains south of Montségur. Montségur was the last stronghold of the Cathar movement in France and it fell after a long siege in 1244. The memories and present-day experiences came over a number of years, with different sequences shown at different times, and after a while I was able to piece together the story. It also became evident, as the story unfolded, that the memories were given to me in order to help me deal with my fears in this lifetime, and to come to terms with what happened then at the time of my passing—since for me it was not at all as White Eagle describes!

I know that I did not go into death 'singing', though many of my compatriots did. Rather, I believe I was supremely afraid. Initially, I think, I led my companions down the twisting path from the castle on Montségur recognizing a tremendous feeling of courage and love which surrounded us all. At this point we did, indeed, sing. Some of us were taken to be burned in the fields below; others, like myself, were walled up in mountain caves. Gradually, as the cold in the cave crept into us, and the air became thinner, I became mortally afraid. The fear grew insidiously within, no matter how much I called on God to help me, and no matter how much I practised my spiritual exercises for such times. It was like a monster which took me over completely in the end, and I believe that I passed to the other side in terror.

White Eagle tells us how what we feel and think in this life we take with us for a time, and I think I began my next stage of life, at the astral level, in shame. Once I became aware of where I was, that deep guilt and remorse was overpowering. Not only had I failed in my ability to overcome my own fear, but I had let my companions down. At a time when they needed me, I could not help them. This was my purgatory—not a God-imposed condition—but one created by my own thoughts about myself.

However, almost at once it was as if I died again—an experience very hard to put into words—it was as if I found myself back at the moment of my transition in the cave. I experienced the great rush of fear, but this time I could feel myself rising upwards on a fountain of energy through grey clouds, and bursting through into the sunlight. I found myself standing in a circle of my brethren from the cave—all of them radiant, forgiving, loving me. Their warmth and sweet understanding surrounded me, melting away all fear and shame. 'We are alive; we understand; there is nothing to be ashamed of; it was all part of the plan for your learning': these were some of their words which echoed inside me.

One important lesson which I feel I am learning from this evolving story in this life, is that whatever happens leads to good. No matter how distressed a person is at the time of their passing, all is taken care of in the most harmonious way for each soul. There may be different experiences for each one of us, but whatever the soul has chosen to go through, the compensation for the suffering is complete. There is a balance in all things, and no-one is left to wander in the darkness of their own fear, pain or guilt, unless by choice. Thus, as you will read from White Eagle in chapter VIII, 'How to relate to those who have passed', there are those who, while they are asleep, help those who have recently passed into spirit life to let go of any residual negativity, and to receive into their being the balm and harmonizing energy which is the divine grace of a God of love. They are helped to move forwards into that love, which is experienced also as light. I feel that I was helped in this way. Our positive and loving waking thoughts towards those who have gone on will aid this process and, if there is need, bring them peace.

Forgiveness

Forgiveness is often difficult, my children; but as soon as forgiveness comes into the heart, there comes release of the spirit; the soul that has been in bondage and perhaps stretched upon the cross of suffering no longer suffers.

Forgiveness has been a part of the teaching of many spiritual traditions; and, as White Eagle says, it is often difficult. Both as a counsellor and as a human being, I frequently encounter the issue of forgiveness! What struck me about White Eagle's words is that he is giving us a reason why forgiveness is crucial to our wellbeing, besides being good for our karma.

Forgiveness is also something which we may need to practise when someone we love is ill. Often, try as we will, we can have feelings of resentment and lack of support, especially if the person who is ill is our partner or parent. In the same way we can feel uncared-for and abandoned by our loved one, and by God, if that loved one dies, however unjust this may feel to another part of ourselves. We may simply be angry with life. No-one likes to admit to these feelings but they are often there. They can be very hard to release, precisely because we do not like to acknowledge their presence.

I imagine that at times most of us have had moments when thoughts about what other people have done to us, or about our misfortunes, simply run away with us. It's a typical thing to happen in the middle of the night, or when we are trying to meditate! At such times it seems as if the mind is quite ungovernable. Transgressions against us can take on enormous proportions, and the people or persons involved become huge and frightening ogres in our minds. We do indeed suffer, as White Eagle says, as if we were suffering from the pain of it all over again, and again. How we long, at such times, to be able to forget!

This can be particularly hard if the person has died, for then their feelings cannot be put into perspective by seeing them again—added to which, our feelings are compounded by guilt. We don't have bad feelings on these occasions because we are stupid or vengeful, but because the limited self is seeking to find a way to understand and then resolve the situation, and thus make the hurt go away. Unfortunately, though, what often happens is that a vicious circle develops which causes us even more distress and resentment.

And the guilt propels the vicious circle. We wish we could respond with love to all the circumstances of life, even when others hurt us. We wish we could love our perceived enemies, and we feel we let ourselves down when we can't. We often feel very badly about reacting with anything but love towards someone who has died, or is terminally ill. Such guilt of itself causes resentment, and thus the limited mind and feelings continue, as White Eagle says, 'in bondage', and stretched upon the cross of suffering.

Before we can move on, we first need to forgive ourselves, and understanding why we react as we do does help. For the simple truth, however difficult it may be to realize, is that when we forgive we really can forget. Until that moment of forgiveness arrives the mind of earth, governed by the hurt feelings underneath, is constantly bringing up the memory of the events which have hurt us.

When we forgive, we have begun the process of letting go. One way to begin to forgive is to acknowledge that we are hurt, but that we are still OK. You can say to yourself, 'It's alright. You are safe.... You are safe and worthy of love and respect, no matter what has happened. You do not need to fight or do anything to make things better'. When you get that message, then the instinct which keeps reminding you of the events that happened is no longer needed. It is similar to the body's response to physical pain. Pain is a useful tool to remind you that you need to do something to save yourself, but once the healing begins, then the body no longer needs to react with pain.

What the instinctive self needs to realize at this earthly level of life is that contact with the divine self is the ultimate healing tool. Forgiveness puts us immediately in contact with the divine self within, and the relief is enormous and instantaneous. This is because when we forgive, our vibrations change. The divine self draws closer. There is a wonderful, strong part of each one of us which is waiting, longing, to draw close and soothe the wounds. When it does, then the earthly self knows it is able to relax its tension. It can then respond to the inner power which is its true life-source. The instinct for self-preservation which is at the root of most resentment and anger is then softened into abeyance, by the inner knowing that the spirit of love is the true protector and source of all strength.

White Eagle reminds us about self-forgiveness in THE QUIET MIND.

Have you ever thought what forgiveness means? You, your own self, your own personality, needs your forgiveness. Your spirit is divine, but until you have overcome, your personality remains human and needs the forgiveness of your spirit. As you forgive, as your spirit forgives your personality, so also you will learn to forgive others for all their seeming errors. If you will train yourself to think in terms of love and forgiveness every moment of your life, a most beautiful healing will take place in you.

Before we come to the personal experience which closes this chapter, I should like to share with you some more Easter teaching which White

Eagle gave once. Here he sought, as ever, to help us understand the great
love in which we are held. He tried to show how even the greatest suffering can be inwardly transformed into peace and joy by our spiritual
contact. In this, of course, Jesus is our greatest example.

We should like to dispel some of the gloom and sorrow which
has been built up and overshadows the Christian world on Good
Friday. This pall of gloom has also been built up in your own
lives. We would have you strive to think of Good Friday, and
your own death, and that of loved ones, as a 'birth', because it
means that the soul is rising to a fuller and more beautiful life.

We do not come to talk to you about the development of
psychic power, or how to hold communication with those who
have passed out of the physical body. We come to show you a
higher way, which, if you will follow it, will obliterate all separation; a way which will throw aside, tear down, the veil of darkness
between you and all life. And when we say all life, we mean the
life of all creation, every kingdom of nature, animal, human
and angelic.

The greatest power to help you is heavenly power, God power;
and the spirit messengers or angels are sent to you for that purpose by the will of God. Do not shut them out. Be calm. Be still.
Do one thing at a time, quietly, tranquilly, and you will make way
in your soul for a great inflow of spiritual power.

We would describe to you, here, on the central altar of your
temple within, a lovely pink rose which is opening its petals to
the sun. A rose is the symbol of the human heart, fragrant with
love. You may not often see hearts like this, but we do. We see
many human hearts open to us, and can inhale the perfume of
sweet human love. You give out that same perfume yourselves.

With this symbol in your midst, be very still. Be at peace....
At this celestial level you will develop the power to receive truth,

the power of feeling and imagination. If you feel the beauty of the heaven worlds, you are receiving divine truth intuitively. This is how you can discriminate between God's will and self-will. *Sell all thou hast, and ... follow me,* Jesus said. Leave your earthly mind, your bodily concerns, your fears for your possessions and your desires, and follow Him.

Know the meaning of the love of God, the brotherhood of all life and the saving power of Christ the Lord. This beautiful pure God–Sun–Spirit comes to recreate and heal you, and to perfect all the rough places in your life. Only surrender to this saving grace, this glorious spiritual power, and you will be healed of all infirmities and sorrows. You will be comforted, and a great peace will come to you.

This is what we would impress upon you. After a period of pain and suffering look forward to the new life, to the rebirth that will come to your heart.

Victory—Kärin

My father died about twenty years ago. I was in my early thirties when he was diagnosed with colon cancer. In the short period of less than three years he went steadily downhill physically, and my husband and I were devastated—we felt much too young to lose him.

It was interesting because, even though I was well-studied in White Eagle's teachings, and had belief in the knowledge that good would come of this, I was facing the loss of my Dad, and my earthly self had a horrid time not wanting to let go. As Dad got more and more sick, I tried to craft my prayers so that I could say, 'Thy will be done', but I always found my mind adding, 'And please don't let him suffer any pain'.

As it turned out, he did suffer greatly, and it made me feel much sorrow. One day I was with him in the hospital as he gradually put the earthly life behind him. The family had made sure there was a fresh bouquet of Birds of Paradise flowers that he could see at the end of his bed. A new vase full of the flowers had arrived that morning, and when I got there he turned his head from his pillow, ever so slightly, to look at me. His voice had been weak, and he had been drifting in and out of sleep for several days. But at this moment my father's eyes were bright, his voice was strong and he seemed filled with energy as he said, 'Did you see Hazel when you came in?'. Hazel was his mother-in-law who had been dead quite a few years. I replied I hadn't see her and asked where she was. He said, 'Right there. Her face was right there'. His head was lifted off the pillow and he was pointing to the vase of Birds of Paradise. 'I saw her right there smiling at me'. I found tears in my eyes and said, 'Oh, Poppy, I'm so glad; do you think she's come to get you?'. And the man that wasn't sure there was any life after death said simply, 'Yes'.

After that time I didn't see him alert again, and a few days later my brother called me and said, 'It's all over'. But I knew it had just started for my Dad. I had wanted, in my little earthly self, for him to suffer no pain, but, at the end, I knew that he had lived his whole life to go through the last three years of his life. If my prayers had been answered in the way I wanted them to be, there would not have been the victory I saw in him, the victory of looking forward to his transition with faith, hope and the certainty that his loved ones would be there to greet him and help him home. He died in peace, and by so doing gave me peace.

Dad comes to me once in a while in my dreams, and we have a great time. I know he lives, is happy, well and encouraging me. Maybe, when my time comes, he'll be the one to come and take me home.

PART THREE: DEATH AND AFTER

VII: THE BRIDGE—LISTENING

WHEN YOU love someone, or when your compassion is aroused by a person's suffering, you long to be able to help them. People like to do things at such times—to feel that they are really making a difference. However, as we learn from the Tao Te Ching, 'Few people realize how much how little will do'.*

Often it is not just the actions of others—the help with shopping and household chores, with the business arrangements, with keeping the lawn tidy (grateful though one is for such acts of consideration) which really make a difference, but the little thing of being there and listening. This is not only because another's presence helps a person not to feel quite so lonely, but because listening is a powerful tool for healing. It creates a bridge for the bereaved person, the one who is dying, or the person who is suffering and afraid, between the past they have known, the present, and their future.

Listening to those who are bereaved

There are many societies in the world where death is a part of living, not one where it is shunned. In parts of India, for example, death is treated in a more natural, and open way. Everyone is encouraged to share in the commemoration of the transition of a community member. However, here in Britain and in America, and in many other Western countries, this is traditionally not so. On the one side there is the tendency not to

*Paraphrase of the Tao te Ching in John Heider's THE TAO OF LEADERSHIP, 1986

talk about death at all, and on the other a fascination with all kinds of death in fiction.

This unhealthy attitude to death has profound effects. A healthy approach to death encourages people to talk about it and to use helpful rituals to deal with it. For the health of our inner being we need the encouragement to expand our horizons and find (inside ourselves, and in nature), the very real evidence of eternal life that is there. Otherwise, we can tend to feel helpless and overwhelmed when faced with someone who is grieving, or our own mortality. Those who are bereaved can be extremely sensitive and are often exhausted. Other people's inability to cope with them and their grief can increase their feelings of abandonment and isolation.

One of the sad things about our own fear of death is that some people find it very difficult to be fully 'present' with a person who is bereaved. To do so can be acutely painful, as it is a reminder of mortality generally. It can also be difficult if we ourselves have had experiences of loss after which we have not grieved properly and completely. Faced with someone who is grieving we can feel the pain of our own experiences again, perhaps without consciously realizing that this is what is happening. Lastly, those who have witnessed life continuing beyond death in a way which is convincing and comforting can, unwittingly, dismiss the pain that another person might be feeling, so that the bereaved person feels even more alone in his or her grief.

Fortunately, the taboos against talking about death have started to break down. There has been much research on the subject, and books written by authors who give encouragement, information and support to the bereaved and the dying, and to those who care for them. In the bibliography there are, among others, two classic studies by Judy Tatelbaum and Elisabeth Kübler-Ross. Through their work with the bereaved and dying, such authors help us learn more about how to listen well.

What strikes me in all my own reading and counselling work is the value of the listening presence to those who grieve, or who are dying. As helpers, we do not need to say much or do much, except to let the person know that we acknowledge their pain, and that we are there with them. It is important to let them talk, to let them cry. It may be that the person is reluctant to open themselves to tears and rage because it seems it would hurt too much to do so. We may then be able gently to help them release, rather than suppress their feelings. It also helps not to be afraid of being on the receiving end of their anger if it comes. Anger may be an expression of hurt. When one is grieving, it can be easier to feel anger than admit the tears and the overwhelming sadness.

There is a range of emotional states and feelings which a bereaved person can feel: from shock (and in some cases, horror) to guilt. I believe that anyone seeking to help a person who is bereaved can feel more secure when they know that these emotions are natural. In knowing this the helper can reassure the person who is experiencing deep emotions that it is quite normal to have that wide range of feelings. Through that reassurance the person is more enabled to move through the emotions we call 'negative' to a place of peace.

Guilt is a most common feeling in those who are bereaved. It is understandable that the person should feel genuine remorse where there have been problems and difficulties with, or even estrangement from, their loved one before death. How many times must it happen that a row occurs just before one partner, child or parent dies, and how painful that must be!

White Eagle encourages the one who is bereaved to talk to the loved one who has passed, even though they are not apparently 'there'. The conversation could be almost like a phone conversation. The other person needs to be strongly created in the imagination. Obviously, someone doing this needs to be balanced about it, and so does a carer in recommending it; yet there comes a natural time in the process of listening, when it may seem just right to approach it in this way. If it feels appropriate to suggest it, the helper might actually lead the person through the exercise on the following page, or offer it to them as something they do for themselves. It is a simple meditation using creative imagination.

In order to grieve completely, people need to be able to explore their feelings all the way through. It is not a good idea to use a technique like this too quickly, in case the person feels one is shocked and embarrassed by their emotions. Eventually the bereaved person comes to the point of letting go. By this I mean consciously changing the way the bereaved might relate to their loved one. The kinds of rituals mentioned in the next chapter, 'How to Relate to Those who have Passed', can be important at this stage. Naturally, most people would love to have some contact with their loved one, in order to know they are alright, and it is tempting on the part of the listener to suggest this too soon. If there are difficult emotions,

---

THE WHITE SEAT

Find a place where you can sit quietly and be undisturbed. Send a thought or prayer to the Great Spirit that you may be guided to make contact with your loved one, and that they may come to you.

Imagine yourself walking into a beautiful garden, arranged just as you would wish. If you cannot imagine something new, then see somewhere you and your loved one have known and loved; perhaps have been to together before.

In this garden is a white seat where you sit and absorb the tranquillity and the gentle sunshine.

Call to your loved one in your heart, and see them walking towards you, looking radiant, and just as they would like you to see them. (Do not worry if the tears flow: it is a natural part of the healing process.)

Not only does your loved one in the world of spirit look as they wish to look, but they are also in their higher self. All the difficulties of the earthly personality, the fears, resentments, criticisms, and so on, which they may have had while on earth, have fallen away, and they are in touch with all the goodness and wisdom of their spirit.

It is in an atmosphere of mutual respect and love that you sit together on the bench. You are enabled to say all the things you want to, including, if this is uppermost in your thoughts, any memories you feel still needs 'sorting out' from the life you have shared, even if they are things you regret.

When the time comes to leave, realize that they will always be there in your heart if you call to them. Come back to an awareness of the physical body slowly, and see yourself surrounded by the strength of the Christ light. Afterwards, it is a good idea to do something which is life-affirming and active.

those need to be heard and released before the bereaved person can truly feel such a contact.

Being with someone who is 'dying'—what to say

Many of us at some stage in our own life will have the privilege of being with someone who is making the transition we call death. I call this a privilege, because that is exactly how others have described it to me, including Irene, whose story is at the end of this chapter. However, to see this experience as a privilege requires a change in the popular conception of the horror of death. Not everyone's transition seems peaceful on the outside, nor is it often welcome. Even so, people who are present at a transition describe, time and again, experiencing a sense of peace and light, or a lovely change coming over the face of the person towards the end. Time and again they say that a death can be a mystical moment. They are speaking of the actual death as an event which transcends all that has gone before—all the pain, anguish and despair—as it literally does. The person is transcendent; they are advancing beyond the confines of the earthly level of consciousness, and finding in that moment that all fear was groundless. They are, we realize, discovering the deepest love. The following passage from White Eagle is a reassuring account of what happens at a passing.

When, as it does to everyone in due course, the time comes for you to lay aside your own physical body, or even to see a loved one of yours withdraw from theirs, don't concentrate your thoughts on that physical body. It disintegrates and goes the way ordained for it by Mother Earth, by Mother Nature. Just above the still form of the one who has passed on, you will see the gates opening. The veil of materialism of the earthly life will be drawn aside. You will see the spirit of your loved one freed to a world of heavenly beauty. You will see him or her overwhelmed with joy to meet loved ones who have long since passed away. Your joy will be in seeing what they have hoped for coming to them. You will see that they meet in a heavenly garden, in heavenly scenery and amid beauty indescribable in earthly language. And more than this, you will see upon their faces the heavenly happiness which fills their hearts when they find that there is no death. There is no death: this is what the master Jesus demonstrated to all human kind. He rose again. Not only in spirit did he rise, but through the power which he had attained by his life, his knowledge of how to raise the physical body, the very atoms of the physical body, into a perfect vehicle. And this the records prove to you, for many people saw Jesus walking along the road. They saw him come into the closed and barred room. They saw him distribute the bread, and invoke the blessing of his Heavenly Father on the food which he distributed to his disciples. You may take these stories as you like, but they were both physical demonstrations of a profound spiritual truth.*

Although we may not be able for ourselves to glimpse what happens at an etheric level as White Eagle describes, nonetheless to be witness to such a process can be moving and transforming; and often it can cut through the pain of the person watching, such is its power. It can even dispel it.

Before those final moments there are other feelings that a helper may have to deal with, both in themselves and in the person who has been told they are going to die. That person may deny this at first, for example. I believe it is important not to challenge this denial, but to respect that this feels to them to be necessary. Quite possibly they are creating a 'breathing space', while their emotions catch up with what the mind is telling them. When we are simply willing to let the person talk it through, without making judgments, gradually they may come to terms with what is happening. This shows immense respect for the person.

*The stories about Jesus after the resurrection are mainly in St John's Gospel, chapter XXI, and in St Luke, chapter XXIV.

In order to feel more in control the person may seek to bargain with God. This may be particularly so if the person has led a spiritual or religious life, and perhaps feels guilty for not being more loving. The cultivation of guilt by a loving God would seems incongruous. It would therefore be the essence of love to help the one who is dying to know that they have always done the best they could. Appreciation and celebration of them as a human being could be very healing.

It is, of course, very easy for someone who is dying to become depressed. I believe that this is one of the hardest emotions to witness, particularly if that person is close to us, and if they have been full of life and spiritual faith. It is hard not to become depressed ourselves as we witness this feeling. Our ability to hold the person, inwardly, in a positive ray of light and joy can be so beneficial for them, and for us, at such times. It is a life-affirming, though inward, response to their distress, and enables the helper to feel they are doing something positive.

Along with intense feelings of isolation, other feelings (guilt, fear, anger and helplessness) can be present in someone who is dying, just as they can be with someone who is bereaved. Our loved one may also be concerned about a number of practical things: whether there will be medication, if they wish it, for the pain; that they will not be left alone (unless they want to be); whether they will be brought home if at all possible and remain there; and whether they will be told everything they want to know. Our loved one or friend may have fears which they are concerned about sharing. If possible, we can ask them what they are most frightened of, to give them a chance to express those fears, and also so that they can be reassured wherever it is possible. Many people are afraid of being a burden to their families, and anxious about how their families will cope when they have gone. People can do much to reassure their loved ones about this, using the kinds of words given in the previous chapter. One feeling in the one who is dying which may be at the root of not wishing to be a burden to others, is hating the thought that they are no longer active, in control, and of use. Again, words of reassurance about how much you still respect and acknowledge the worth of the person can help. Remember that listening to how hard it is to feel so helpless and useless—giving the

SHARING THE FINAL MOMENTS

If you can, hold the hand of your loved one who is awaiting transition as you sit with them.

Think of your love for them, and allow that love to flow from you to them. Imagine, then, that they are bathed in a strong, brilliant ray of light, which is the perfect divine love.

This light is healing, and brings clarity to the mind and peace to the emotions.

Imagine this ray enveloping and interpenetrating their whole body, mind and emotions. Where it touches any dark clouds of depression, they are dissolved.

See your loved one then as their higher self—radiant and full of joy.

You may keep this thought of your loved one bathed in healing light in your mind at any time while you are with them, but also you could deliberately think of it before you go to sleep and when you wake in the morning.

person permission to share their hardest thoughts and feelings—will do much to bring relief.

It is a great temptation to run away from our loved one's pain, because it is so very hard to be in a situation where, while we listen, we feel helpless about what to say or do. The one who is dying is often also seeking to protect those around him or her from too much grief; and yet inside there may be fears and sorrow which he or she is longing to share with others. Quite often there will be hospital counsellors, for example, who could give this support: but if not, the greatest gift we can give our loved one is our loving listening—our preparedness to listen to their deepest longings and heartache.

The person may also be in a great deal of pain, and on medication. Both pain and medication can have the effect of dulling the senses, and making it harder to focus. Medication can make one depressed. It may therefore be harder than usual, even for someone who does have faith and awareness of the spirit, in such circumstances, to hold on to their

spiritual understanding. They may find it very difficult to meditate or attune themselves, at just the time it could be most useful.

What a good listener can do is to hear how difficult it is, without despair. It is extremely hard to listen to someone who has been sure of life
after death seeming to lose their faith. What the carer can eventually do
is to be the dying person's bridge to the other world, both by their loving listening, but also by leading them in inspiring, guided meditations
which take them across the divide from one level of consciousness to the
other. These guided meditations should not be too long. They should be
beautiful, and involve someone at the next level of consciousness who can
greet the dying person when they arrive. But if you are the caregiver, the
more you can make ordinary in them the better. You are simply building
a bridge. White Eagle tells us that, at first, the one who has made the
transition does not know they have died. Everything is as it would be on
earth, except perhaps that the atmosphere where they are is full of love
and light. Gradually the realization is brought home to the one who has
died in a way which is gentle and not shocking. What you can be assured
of, he seems to be saying, is that what you imagine—at those times when
you are helping your dying friend to find the bridge—is absolutely true and
real, and even more beautiful than you can describe. The angels of death,
and the dying person's loved ones in spirit, will be creating the bridge from
their side. They will impress you with what to say, and with the feelings of
love and peace which will best help the one who is in need.

It is, of course, important to treat the dying person with respect and
naturalness and to be full of hope and trust, for the quality of their life is
important all the way through. The more that one can be natural, with
all the humour and lightness of touch which one would usually have, and
yet prepared to listen at all times, the more the dying person will feel safe.
In a sense, we are demonstrating for them the faith which they can have
in their continued existence as the person they are, as well as the greater
soul and spirit they are going home to be.

White Eagle, in a well-known passage in his book, THE GENTLE BROTHER,
illustrates the quality of listening which truly helps others, by describing
how a master soul would listen to someone.

Forget everything else but your companion as you are conversing with him or her. Concentrate your whole attention on what is being said. Courtesy at least demands this. If the Master should come and you, not knowing it was he, talked to him—possibly foolishly—the Master would take notice of your every word. For the time being your conversation would be all that mattered to Him.

In due time our loved one may come to a degree of acceptance, as in a number of the stories given here, although this may not always happen. Our most loving response is to accept them, no matter what. Acceptance above all may cut through possible feelings of isolation.

Eventually, when the moment of death is near, the level of consciousness changes for the person; their etheric body is rising 'above' the physical, as recounted by many who have had near-death experiences, as well as by teachers like White Eagle.* Also, they are being welcomed into the light by those whom they recognize and love. This is the moment when those who are watching, from the earth level of consciousness, can send their loved one forward with encouragement and joy. Even verbally and out loud we can speed them on their way and help the pull of the earth-consciousness to lessen and set them free. If that is not possible, they will hear words spoken in the silence of our heart with conviction and love.

Of course you will not find that the person passes immediately you do this, unless you are quite certain of your timing, and you may witness them still in distress in the physical body. But at another level, White Eagle assures us, they will be responding to this affirmation, and you will be creating a stronger and more accessible bridge for them to that next level of life.

Another spirit guide, Emmanuel, in one of his books, says:

> To help someone die in peace, remind yourself—
> and him—that he is going Home,

*One of White Eagle's descriptions of this occurs in the next chapter. See the paragraph beginning 'Angels encompass the one about to leave his or her physical body' on p. 144.

that he is leaving illusion and moving back into truth.
You have all experienced dreams that you knew
were not the usual sleeping dreams.
You have gone somewhere wonderful,
soft, loving, joyful, and lighted.
Believe those dreams. Encourage your dying friend
to believe in his own dreams.
They are visits Home.

LETTING THEM GO

As you hold your loved one's hand, or sit by them, speak to them in your heart.

See them on the threshold of a passageway of light, or any similar image which comes to you. Maybe the image will be one which would mean something in particular to the person.

Silently give them permission to go forward towards those who wait joyously for them at the end of the passage.

You may feel very sad, but tell your loved one that you let them go—that you want them to be happy and you know that just a little way further on they will experience real joy and release from pain and fear.

Tell them you will always be with them on an inner level, and that you, and those they leave behind, will be fine.

Tell them you will see them on the other side in your quiet times, and when you sleep.

Reassure them of the continued relationship you both share, perhaps an even deeper one than before, and invite them to step forwards into a place of great loveliness, where they will instantly feel at home and deeply loved. Describe such a place for them—one which you know they will love.

Then see your loved one moving down this passageway of light into a greater light—towards freedom, happiness and all the things they may have longed for on earth.

Helping someone's passing, through healing—Irene

Last weekend I had the privilege of being able to go on giving healing and support to one of my patients right up to the moment when she passed on, and this raised a number of questions in my mind about the best ways to help dying patients—accepting, of course, that each one will be different in many respects. I simply had to follow my own intuitions.

I had started giving healing to Sylvia in the summer, when she had been given my name by the local Cancer Support Group. I had visited her twice a week since then—more than twenty times—each time staying about an hour, so I had got to know her very well. We found we had a lot in common and, herself a Quaker, she understood the concept of spiritual healing from the very start and was not necessarily seeking a cure. We talked openly about death and the afterlife, and I know that she looked forward to my visits, whether at her home or in hospital, as they sometimes were. This close bond was respected by her family and they wanted me to be with her at the end, as they trusted me by this time to sit alone with her for many hours while they took a much-needed break. In the last day of her life I was with her for about ten hours, sometimes alone, sometimes with others.

Inevitably I longed to help her to pass on easily. But how best to do this? All our training is aimed at healing the spiritual body in order to reach the physical body. But as her death became imminent I moved my concentration mainly to the spiritual.

Until four days before her death I gave Sylvia the normal White Eagle healing treatment for cancer, with the particular colours prescribed for her condition. During the last day, however, I felt quite sure that my job was simply to help her passing and the following describes what I did. I must make clear that during this time she was unconscious, in hospital, breathing with great difficulty and that the doctors expected her to die at any moment.

I gave blue to all the chakras for the pain (though morphine was also being administered for this), for peace, and to aid the transformation through death. Certainly it had a calming effect which was noted even by the family. Right at the end, an hour or so before death, I visualized the chakras completely still, like beautiful blue flowers, but totally motionless. It was a powerful image.

Sitting there for hour after hour I realized, yet again, as a healer the patience and humility we need to accept that the timing is not for us to control. All as God wills.

Talking gently for hour after hour to someone who seems unconscious but who may well be able to hear, I found certain White Eagle phrases recurring again and again in my mind. They seemed to say exactly what I wanted to communicate, which are more or less paraphrases of sentences from the services of healing in the White Eagle Lodge.

'Close your senses to the outer world. Lay aside all the thoughts of the earth which trouble and imprison you, and seek communion with the inner world, the world of spirit and eternal life, the real world.' I also found myself saying, 'Do not fear that you can ever be really separated from your loved ones here. You will still be here in our midst, nearer than breathing, closer than hands and feet … a sister to our innermost, for in perfect love there can be no separation'.

Apart from giving colours, I spent many hours in visualizing with my patient, at first keeping to one image, which was a bridge of light that she could cross little by little at her own pace. Then later, when I realized that I had more time, I used other images that occurred as I meditated beside her. The most vivid was a tidal inlet on a sunlit beach, from which the tide had gone right out leaving the sands wet and wrinkled and easy to walk across into the sun … to a bright, tree-covered shore beyond.

Then when she seemed to me more sleepy and less conscious, I felt in meditation very compassionate and motherly towards her, though of course not in the least in a patronizing way to such a strong and enlightened soul. It was like sitting beside a much-loved baby who can't sleep, and I envisaged lifting her gently and tiptoeing with her over to the other side and handing her over to waiting arms. As she too was a very loving mother, I felt she would appreciate being mothered herself for once.

I envisaged, and described to her too, the angels who were gathering, especially the beautiful angel of death, who was also, it seemed to me, a mother-figure in a deep blue robe.

In the last half hour, as we all watched in silence round her bed, thinking every breath was her last, in my own heart I particularly asked White Eagle to help release her, if it was God's will, and I 'saw' him and a beautiful Red Indian woman lift her lightly, wrapped in a blue shawl of light, and carry her off still sleeping. Soon after that her breathing changed, grew weaker and shallower and stopped.

Finally, a practical hint. If the family agree, take along a cassette recorder with lovely quiet music. Someone had done this and I certainly appreciated it as well as Sylvia!

VIII. HOW TO RELATE TO THOSE WHO HAVE PASSED

ONE OF THE comforting opportunities to change our perception which is given us by White Eagle is the promise of a continued relationship with our loved ones. Since life is continuous and one whole, our relationship with them, though obviously changed by the death of the body, is ongoing.

The next few sections begin with remarks from White Eagle about the eternal links we have through our love one for another. 'At the Moment of Transition', 'The Importance of Ritual', and the sections on 'Grieving' and the chapter entitled 'The Comforter', which follow, all deal with this changed relationship and how we are helped to come to terms with it.

We want to help you to understand that where there is love, real love, there is no separation; because in that love you all are united at a certain level; and at that same level, as we have already said, the communion of saints becomes a real thing.

Your loved ones, when they pass away, may for a time (according to their nature) be rather tied to earth. Because they have recently left the body they miss it, and they remain to all intents and purposes exactly the same person as before. Because they lack a physical body, they cannot touch or speak to you; neither can you touch them nor speak to them in a physical way. But otherwise they are exactly the same as they were. In a very short time, however—it may be two or three hours, days, weeks, for we do not measure time in your way—the soul is helped (if it needs to be) by its own guide and teacher. The teacher explains that the individual is not really separated from his or her loved ones.

We would like you to realize also that you can be extremely active in your astral body in the spirit world without knowing it. You may be actually engaged in certain material work and be unaware that you have been visiting a sick friend or a relative at a distance. You may have even been seen by that relative or loved one, and be unaware of it. You will learn in time of this. At present you are confined, we were going to say, in a three-dimensional world and are largely unaware of any of your spiritual activities, either in your sleep state or during meditation.

At the moment of transition

In the following passages, White Eagle gives us further help with understanding the nature of our new relationship with our loved one after their death. Through a number of descriptions given at different times and in response to the needs of his listeners, he explains what is actually happening at the moment of transition from one level of life to another.

We want you to remember that there is no death. This perhaps sounds peculiar when we tell you, but when you come face to face with the sorrow and grief of parting with a physical body of a dearly-loved friend, you forget that there is no death, and you are inclined to centre all your thoughts upon that physical shell which is finished, and has been shuffled off.

Yet in the spirit world there is the most perfect plan for the reception of every soul who leaves a physical body. A messenger is sent to welcome the newly-released soul from the physical body, to welcome them into a world of peace and beauty, a spiritual beauty such as you cannot understand.

It is true that there comes a time in the evolution of the soul when the soul has to face up to certain lessons. Every soul must learn, and learn by its own experience. So, in the spirit world (when the time is ripe, and only then) the soul is very kindly and tenderly shown pictures of its own life. And from these pictures the truth dawns upon the man or woman. The soul can see by that object-lesson where it failed, where it missed its opportunity while on earth. The soul may feel deeply regretful, but gets further help from its teacher or companions in spirit, and is cheered and reassured. The soul is given strength and courage, and learns of the wisdom and mercy of God.

When you see, in the outer world, violence and what appears to be the most terrible suffering, brought about by the ignorance and the selfishness of human kind, do remember the mercy of God and the power of God. The soul that is apparently leaving a tortured body is mercifully cloaked by a divine power. Inside, it is filled with indescribable joy and surprise: 'Oh, this is wonderful, this is beautiful, where am I, where am I?'. And the friend by his or her side will answer: 'You are with friends; we have so much of interest to show you'. Then that soul is led away to objects which are familiar, but beautiful. So you see, from our side of life death is nonexistent; all is living eternally in that divine Love; that great Light; that divine Intelligence.

Make no mistake about it, every soul who comes over to our life is befriended. It does not matter who he or she is, or what harm they have done; or how wrong they may have been according to earthly standards. That soul is welcomed by a friend, one who really gives love. Many come back to those on earth with the same message: 'It is so beautiful over here. We have found peace'. But remember this, that after the soul has been befriended, then the healing has to take place. 'Heal thyself', you have been told: so you see that all healing comes from within your own being, but you are helped by the healers and teachers which come to you.

You have within you the power of God, which will enable you to comprehend all these glories. You must release yourself from death. And this physical life is death, or is imprisonment, *but you are not bound to live in a closed cell.* You can open the windows of your cell. You can let the walls of your cell disintegrate, and you can be free in the life of God.

*

When death draws near, angels always gather in the home of the one about to depart. You may think of the Angel of Death as an angel of darkness and terror, but you are wrong. The Angel of Death is like the Holy Mother, all love and tenderness, gentleness and beauty. When a soul receives the call from earth to heaven, loving preparation is made in the spirit world for the reception of that soul. If only people could have their vision clear enough to see that welcome being made ready, they would never be sad at death; they would be as happy—indeed more happy—than when a child is born into life down here.

Angels encompass the one about to leave his or her physical body. The spirit about to be freed rises from that body through the head. It rises as you can rise in your meditations, but without the dull pull which you all feel from the body left behind. The cord by which the spirit is attached to the heart is severed, and then the spirit is free and borne on angels' wings. Usually the soul body, being rather denser than it will be later on, passes out through some open window or door and is accompanied by angels to its new home, where all is made ready. Once there, the soul is laid gently on a soft couch facing what you would call open windows, or a space in the room open to the air. The perfume of flowers from the garden of the home steals in. In the reception room or chamber where the spirit lies resting, those who love that dear one are waiting. As soon as its consciousness awakens, the new arrival is greeted by someone beloved and familiar. Remember that there is always someone who loves waiting in the spirit world for those who pass on; no-one journeys from the earth to the world of spirit without meeting with a loving welcome, because every living soul has some loved one in the world of spirit.

What of the dear ones left behind to mourn their loss? Angels are with them also, and bring to their earthly friends a spiritual food which can sustain and give them strength. So long as those who mourn can and will rise above self-pity and think only with tender love and rejoicing of the soul which has passed into the light, then such ones on earth are fed by the light and love of God's messengers.

It is the materiality and shadow of the earth mind which causes pain and grief. You can prove this for yourselves when you tune into the realms of light, when all burdens will slip away. When you are functioning in full consciousness in that higher world you will have no burdens. You will know happiness, for you are in a state of happiness. And so, my children, you will learn from this that happiness—heaven—is within the soul.

*

When it happens that those people who have no knowledge of the spirit life are suddenly flung out of physical life—maybe blown to pieces, or crashed to the earth and injured beyond description, we want you to know that they are instantly taken care of. When they walk out of their body they do not know what has happened to them. But they walk out and find someone, a friend, waiting for them. When they come to themselves (that is, when the etheric body has very rapidly come together, been built up), should they find themselves in a state of confusion or darkness it will be only for a brief, brief span. Almost before they know it, someone is there.

We should like you to picture this: in the spirit world there are—shall we say?—many centres of service. There is an infinity of helpers who are sent out by their master to help. You would be surprised if you could see the way the spirit world is organized for the help of souls, souls on the physical plane and souls on the plane immediately beyond the physical life, who may be in a state of darkness.

Every one of these souls is known. Do you remember Jesus saying that not a sparrow falls to the ground, *without your Father?* And *the very hairs of your head are all numbered?* And so it is. From these centres of service there is sent forth a group, or groups, of ordinary men and women. According to the needs of the soul who is in a place of darkness, so the helper is chosen, the right kind of helper, the helper who can most easily or readily get into communication with the soul who is being helped.

Think of this, and if you have at any time had cause to be doubtful or anxious about anyone you love—anyone who has, either through war or accident, been flung into the spirit world—and you wonder what happened to them, never forget these faithful servers, who move together, in groups, carrying the light, going into the dark places.

Many times people on earth who are bereaved will have received messages from spirit which say: 'I was caught up in a light' or 'I saw a light, a blessed light in the darkness, and it moved, and I followed it'. As they followed that light they would have very soon found friends, kindly friends waiting to give them exactly what they most needed at that time.

We want you to understand that the world of spirit is very natural, very normal in all the things which the lower etheric of a person still wants (because for a while he or she still retains desires of the flesh) and a comforting meal might be heaven to some soul who has just left the physical body. All these things, good things, are prepared for him or her.

*

We want to tell you this, that at the beginning of our mission on the earth plane we were given a charge. We were told that our work on your earth plane was to help to remove from the mind the mad fear of death; and this is the purpose of our mission, to help you all to banish every fear of death you might have. Now, you are fearful of the unknown, not only the unknown in the world of spirit, but your own unknown future. You are fearful of all that you do not know and all that you do not understand. We come only to open little shutters in your mind, give you a little glimpse here and there of the truth of spirit life, the truth about the journey upon which you are set. On this journey of life, of evolution, you are sent forth, you are planted in the dark earth. For many of you it is a very dark soil, but where you are planted in the earth is entirely dependent upon yourself.

There is a divine law which directs this evolution of life through physical matter and part of that law is the law of reincarnation. The law of reincarnation means that you have to go through school. You are taken next through the various classes into college, into the university, and eventually you are initiated into the glories of God's world. How can you, at the beginning of this journey, understand what awaits you in the future?

Nevertheless, you have had planted within you (as it were in the dark earth) a seed, a golden seed; and the purpose of your life is to nurture that seed, help it to grow and blossom. All these beauties which you are enjoying now in your physical life will all develop and increase to a very high degree when you have passed your tests and are free in the cosmos.

*

Can you comprehend freedom, freedom from all want and limitation, freedom from evil thoughts, freedom from pain? Can you imagine yourself free to give and share with all creatures and all human beings this wonderful life of God? The great initiate Jesus, the Christed one, has demonstrated to you that there is a life beyond the physical body, a life beyond death. You will remember the words written in your bible in which the woman said, finding the stone rolled away from the tomb: *They have taken away my Lord.* The stone is the mortal mind, the material mind, and that stone has to be removed. You are in your own tomb in a physical body, but the ministering angel comes to you and will remove the stone, enabling you to rise and come out of your physical body into a world of infinite beauty. And the voice bewailed, *They have taken away my Lord, and I know not where they have laid him.* Now this is what you feel when you have lost a loved one. Where has she gone? Where has he gone? Where has my darling child gone? But the Master returned and explained that he had not died. He had not been taken away, he was still there with them.

This is the most beautiful illustration of what you call death, or the passing of the soul from one condition, of one state of life, to the next. It is to this next world that the soul goes for refreshment and rest, and absorption of those things of the spirit which maybe it had glimpsed while in the tomb, but could not reach because the mortal mind was blocking the way. You may see an inanimate form lying there, but the spirit is freed, is alive, is able to overcome all the limitations of time and space.

*

There is doubt in the mind, fear about the actual passing out of the tomb into that heavenly state of life. But we wish to reassure you that if you surrender yourselves in quietness, in trust to the Great Spirit, there is nothing to fear, but everything in which to rejoice. You think of being a prisoner on earth and then having the prison gate flung open, and out you go into the wide, wide life. We will tell you, as far as we are allowed, what happens when the transition takes place from the physical body. Your loved one may appear to have a little struggle, or may not appear to have any struggle at all, but if there is a little struggle for breath, it does not affect your loved one. They are released from the physical body, they are borne on angel wings, or in the arms of the angels who are waiting for them; and they are carried away to the spirit world, and there they may be taken to a beautiful blue lake. Sometimes it is called the blue country because the atmosphere, the air, seems to be like the sky: blue, so clear, so fresh.

And when they awaken from their sleep, their angel guide is with them, and they are told that if they wish they may take a plunge into that blue lake. Indeed, they are told they will feel better if they take a bathe. So almost invariably the urge is so great, they have a beautiful swim in that blue lake; and it means that they are cleansed and purified of all earthly entanglements and unpleasant things. They are freed, cleansed, purified. Then they rest for a time on the green bank, which is dotted with flowers. They see God; they understand that they are looking into God's world, seeing the life, the real life.

The colours in the world of spirit are not dull like your colours. To us, your colours are very dull; but in the world of spirit nature, the trees, the flowers, even the very air itself, pulsates with colour, intensified colour. Our colours are not aggressive, but most harmonious; and the colours that we see in the spirit world have their vibration of harmony so that the colours are also music, the grand orchestra of infinity. This is what your loved ones go to. This is what you yourself will eventually reach.

My mother's experience—Astra

My mother and I were very close and, apart from one year in America, I had always lived with her. In the last few years of her life she suffered from a heart condition and very high blood pressure. Because of this the consultant admitted her to hospital to try and regulate it. Towards the third day of her stay there I was on my way to visit her when I was suddenly gripped in the chest and felt as if something had knocked me. I instinctively knew it wasn't my problem, and I glanced at my watch and saw it was noon. After a while the tightness in my chest eased and I continued on to the hospital. On arrival I went straight to my Mum's room and saw she wasn't there. One of the nurses told me Sister had been trying to ring me, because my mother had a heart attack and had been taken to intensive care at noon. She did not regain consciousness.

Some time after in meditation Mum came to me, looking lovely and so bright. I wanted to know how she felt about her passing. She explained that she had felt a pain in her chest when the nurse was taking her blood pressure, and that was the last thing she remembered. The next thing was that she woke up and was still in a bed. She showed me what she saw: that she was still in a room with three walls but on the right side there was no wall at all but rather a clear opening, looking out onto lovely trees, greenery and shrubs. She thought it was all so beautiful.

Then she realized that my father was next to her (he had passed into spirit twenty-four years previously) and thought immediately she must be dreaming. My father then took her hand and started speaking to her. She was surprised as his hands felt absolutely real. She said he looked handsome and cheerful. When she asked what was happening he told her that she had left her old life and had joined him. My mother was upset that she had left me on my own, even though it was lovely to be with him.

After a while Mum's eldest brother, whom she had been very fond of, joined them, and together they tried to calm Mum down. Eventually they asked her to watch the wall opposite. She said it was like a cinema screen, and suddenly pictures came on it of how my life would evolve, which reassured her that I would be fine.

Finally, my Dad took Mum away and pointed her towards the greenery and the trees. He walked with her for a little while. Then in the distance a beautiful being of light came towards her. I felt that, to my mother, this would have represented Jesus, as she was a very devout Catholic. My father stopped and bade her go on; whereupon she was embraced by this beautiful being, going on and disappearing into the light.

The importance of ritual

White Eagle also has useful teaching about the moments after death for those remaining on earth, and the rituals we go through at those times.

When a person is released from the physical body, it is not such a terrible thing as you who are living on earth think it is. A door opens and a soul goes out into a world of light. At all events the soul feels light, because it has dropped a physical body which is very heavy, maybe a body which is riddled with pain. Think of being released from a prison. As an example, consider the change which takes place when the insect, the dragonfly, shuffles off the case of the chrysalis and rises into the sunshine with beautiful coloured wings.

We give you this picture to help you understand the feeling of the soul which is released from the body, and for this reason we like to see a committal service which is like a service of light, of joy. We like to witness a service of thanksgiving to God for the release of the prisoner. After the soul has left the body, there should be thanksgiving to God for the great love which God folds around His–Her child who is released from the physical body.

We can be encouraged by White Eagle having said that contact is not lost with those whom we love. Yet we, and others like us, may not always be aware of the contact to be made. There may be other sources of sadness too. So often one of the greatest sorrows for someone who is bereaved is the thought of not doing things together with their loved one any more. This lack of contact is very hard, even though they may have faith that in the future they will once more be with the one they love.

Rituals can play an important part in healing this sadness. As well as adapting exercises given earlier (such as the one on p. 130) for moments before the time of death, you could sit with your loved one in your imagination and celebrate your life together—remembering all the good times and giving thanks for them. This may involve going to a special earthly place as well, and involve an outward ceremony. Not only do these rituals help to establish changes of awareness and relationship with the person who has gone on, but they also help the person who is bereaved to establish new experiences together with their loved one. These rituals can help give faith that the experience of life together goes on and on, albeit in a different form—that death does not separate where love links two souls.

The Memory House—Stuart

In the Palani Hills in South India there are many small villages accommodating very poor people, whose principal religion is Hinduism. When somebody dies the family sit the person in a chair, and all those who are close to the deceased will visit, pay their respects and garland the body with flowers. At sunset, usually on the same day, the men of the village will carry the body and chair on a litter to the earth grave, singing and chanting along the route. The eldest son will lead the procession six times around the grave. After this the body is lowered into the earth, sometimes lying down, sometimes sitting and occasionally even standing. The family members lead the ritual of throwing the earth onto the body and the grave is finally topped by the garlands that have been presented earlier in the day.

Most villages have put aside a special piece of land and built on this an open structure which consists of a thatched roof supported by wooden or stone pillars. This is the Memory House. At dawn on the day after the funeral the villagers will gather sitting beneath this roof. Led by the elders and speaking in turn people will talk about the dead person, recalling childhood, achievements, adventures and sorrows. This respectful process will continue, sometimes for several hours, until all have had their say and the memory is exhausted.

The Memory House is used only for this purpose. The grief, as well as the love for the person, and the respect for his or her life, is visibly shared by all in attendance. This has the effect of binding these materially poor and hard-working people closely together as a mutually supportive spiritual unit.

Ritual can help at the deepest soul level. Ritual often involves doing things which would seem to achieve nothing. When performed with awareness, however, these rituals can have a powerful effect on the atmosphere: that is, the psychic arena in which we live, and on the emotions of all involved. Rituals are often creative on the etheric level, and therefore affect not only us, but those who have gone on. This explains the added importance of the kind of ritual that frees the astral body from restraints and ties to the immediate past life, and lets it move on from the place and moment of death. There is a form of service in the White Eagle Lodge which does precisely this.

White Eagle described, in the previous section, how the one who has died is often taken to a 'blue lake' to be cleansed of ties to the conditions of earth. Deliberately 'imagining' this taking place for one's loved one can help them—at a time when the ties to earth are strongest—to move quickly through this period of releasing into the beauty of the spiritual life. It can also help the one on earth to feel that they are remaining a part of the person's existence, yet in a positive, freeing way; that they are still able to do something for them. This can be very healing.

Rituals can also release those left behind from being caught up in the memory of the death, or the appearance of the person at the end of their life. The ritual gives the bereaved a chance to reconnect with the person as they once were, in their prime—which is just how they will be in the afterlife.

As they would wish to be seen—Colum

When I first started working at the White Eagle Lodge in London, among our patients there was an elderly man who we for a long time knew simply by his surname. This was unusual, for most patients like to be named from the outset by their first name, and in some ways it helps the healing process when the whole name can be brought into focus. But Gerald—as I only later discovered his name to be—was one of those rather private people whom you don't quickly get to know, even though you develop an affection for them, as we all did. He used to call me 'father', which was quite inappropriate, but we were able to laugh about it, and he travelled quite a long distance to get to us, always in a shabby raincoat and carrying the same plastic carrier bag—which as the weeks went by got grubbier and grubbier.

Because of the distance, and the privacy he buttoned around himself, no-one knew much about his circumstances, and it was really difficult to offer the level of active pastoral care we might have offered to someone living within our closer catchment area. He came faithfully week after week, and although he had a severe form of cancer, his final deterioration was not very obvious until he did not return after one of our recess periods. It was not entirely a shock to learn of his passing when it came, but it was a shock to have a letter from a relative which was full of agonizing guilt that his family had not exerted themselves more about his condition: on his death certificate the cause of death was given as malnutrition (though this may have been aggravated by the disease).

I hope we have ourselves learnt from this episode that active watchfulness is needed, even though there were plenty of medical bodies whose responsibility for his material care was more immediate than ours. In the short term, however, I had not only my own feelings to deal with but also those of his sister, who was deeply upset at the way in which she felt she had 'failed'.

And so we come to the touching part of the story. When I was replying to her (I think second) letter, quite without trying and without any knowledge of his history, I became aware of a man apparently rather taller than

Gerald standing before me in the uniform of one of the Armed Forces. He stood straighter than I ever remembered him before. He looked radiantly proud of his condition and appearance. There was not a hint of regret, only of absolute confidence in life and of happiness.

Of course I communicated this to his sister—very nervously, for I was quite unused to having visions in this way. It turned out to be exactly what she needed to know and hear. Not only was there the reassurance that he was 'well' but, as she said, the only time in his life that Gerald ever felt confident and good about himself was in his Forces days. She now had a wholly new conception of how he was. It was as a result totally convincing for her, and very healing.

Another effect of rituals can be to free the mourner from being overwhelmed by painful feelings. This state is not a selfish, negative state which the person wants to be in, but can often be caused by the links between the one who has passed and the one left behind. For example, if the bereaved had been looking after the one who has passed on for a long time, perhaps through a painful illness, their etheric bodies could have become somewhat intertwined. This often happens where there is some kind of negative emotional link, perhaps resentment or guilt; or some anger or fear. When it is more a positive link, then there is less holding-on by the lower astral body and consequently the mourning is more straightforward.

Any ritual has to mean something, and must do so for all experiencing it, but primarily for the family and friends. Therefore it is important that at one level it should be as uniquely personal as possible, although using a more impersonal form of service, or liturgy, may provide an outer strength and framework which is helpful. Any cremation or burial service which can be adapted to the needs of the mourners, and truly express how they feel, will be helpful. A service like this will celebrate the life of the one who has passed on. It can make a link between the past and the future, so that all present can feel their continuing relationship with their loved one. It will ideally involve some ritual which has significance for

NOTES FOR A POSSIBLE SERVICE AFTER SOMEONE'S PASSING

Consider the following elements.

◊   The person taking the service would do well to acknowledge the feelings of those in need of comfort.

◊   Give an opportunity for a time of reflection when although those feelings may remain, nonetheless the words of the service may lift the mourners out of their sorrow, and allow them to catch a glimpse of the eternal nature of life. This may be done best by a prepared silence.

◊   Celebrate the life of the person, and if it feels right, include sensitively humorous moments, that can cause smiles among the tears, and enable the mourners to remember the person as they were in their best moments. A focus on life as it manifested in them may help to give a sense of continuity with how they are now.

◊   Offer a moment where the people present consciously release the one they love into their new life. This would include words of committal which could help the mourners not to hold on to what is mortal, and enable the soul of the person who has passed to lose any attachments to the earth which may be unhelpful.

◊   At the end it is nice to offer a blessing upon the arisen soul, and upon all those remaining, leaving them with a feeling that their relationship each to each continues on, even though it is changed in form.

the onward journey of the soul—a freeing of the ties to earth, as well as a strengthening of the bonds of love.

A service for the arisen soul of someone who has passed which meets the needs of those who attend needs certain elements, but can be immensely helpful if sensitively arranged. To help in this, I have set out some notes above. There are also other rituals which those who are mourning can go through, both in the period just after bereavement, and at significant times afterwards, an example being at particular anniversaries. People often do not imagine until it happens to them that all the dates of anniversaries associated with the relationship carry a particular poignancy, for the first year especially.

'A Spiritual Bouquet'—Dave

(Isabella was born to Dave and Christy Pratt just before Christmas, 2001; she lived only a day. This was Dave's moving speech at Isabella's funeral.)

I have agonized over whether I should try to write anything down for today, December 22nd, 2001. At first, I felt that the only thing I could do before this group of loved ones would be to stand before you, press my palms together, and bow. Then I would turn and do the same towards this beautiful little baby. I thought anything more would be too much. A simple bow acknowledges and honours all of Isabella Virginia Pratt's short life and death, and our connection to her.

I now find I am not able to rest with just that gesture; I feel that Christy, Hannah, Isabella and I need to spell out exactly what has happened and is happening. Never in our lives has any event been simultaneously so wonderful and so horrifically painful.

The wonder of our daughter is her uniqueness, her unbelievably powerful definition of the fact that all life here is temporary. It is because of the fleeting, impermanent nature of life that it is so special, which we often forget or take for granted. Isabella is a rare gem in this universe, as is every person in this room. Due to our brief, intense time with her, we are all changed forever. The sacredness of every moment that we have the privilege of experiencing, good or bad, is harder to forget.

Our daughter had a condition known as Thanatophoric Dysplasia, an obscure form of dwarfism that is terminal for all of these children. Babies like her arrive on an average of only 1 in 40,000 to 45,000. All die soon after birth. The name itself makes things clear. It translates from Greek as 'Moving towards death'. Once again, there is no survival rate, regardless of whether the baby is at full term or not. The rarity of cases makes it difficult, if not impossible, to predict, even with today's modern marvels. Of course, Christy and I are not concerned that we had no prior knowledge of her condition from doctors. I'm simply telling you the facts so you know the exact truth. The most crucial factor that results in death for these babies is the pronounced underdevelopment of the lungs. They cannot expel enough carbon dioxide from their bodies to remain alive very long outside the womb.

This may sound odd, but I have only recently realized that many of the tears I am shedding are for all of you, in addition to Isabella and my wife, Christy, and daughter, Hannah. It is a strange, blooming wound to lose a child and know that she came here and did exactly what she intended at exactly the right time. We grieve our little girl as we grieve your suffering. Mother Theresa once said (I'm paraphrasing): 'I know God won't give me more than I can handle. I just wish he didn't trust me so much'. To me, that concisely encapsulates the events of the last few days.

At the beginning of writing these words, I said that we've never known anything before to be so wonderful and horrifically painful. I wanted to make sure to explain why I believe Isabella's life was a wonderful gift, a gift to break our hearts and let all the love that exists come rushing out. The pain is obvious and needs no explanation. This little girl was not an accident or a mistake. Her perfection is indubitable. Her strength, determination and sacrifice to stay with us long enough to say goodbye to her mother, is a miracle.

Not long after her arrival, doctors asked that she be taken to Akron Children's Hospital to confirm their suspicions that she did indeed have Thanatophoric Dysplasia. We were told that even with life support, there was a very good chance she would not survive the journey. However, she did survive—all the way until the following afternoon when we brought her back home here to Millersburg, where she died in our arms. We cannot thank her enough. She breathed the same air we now breathe, under the same sun and moon. Like the air, she is now present around and within us. A part of her is with all of us to take along on our personal journeys.

For the last few days, you have all been asking or wondering what you could do for Christy, Hannah and I. We know that you would do anything and we love you all. Your presence here today is the second greatest gift we have ever received, but because I am human, I am going to ask more of you.

Meditate or pray on what this one-day-old teacher has taught you and let her live through you. Share this lesson in an everyday act of kindness or caring that arrives unexpectedly, perhaps to a stranger, perhaps to yourself or someone else. Figure out how the wonder of this child can illuminate your own or someone else's life. Imagine a planet of warriors strong enough to cry, persistent and forgiving enough to love their enemies, and awake enough to take nothing for granted. Try to treat yourself with the same loving kindness, compassion and non-judgmental care that you receive from your God and perhaps ache to give away to others. Remember that the idiosyncrasies of all those on this planet are what makes us each a wonder. They are often keys into another's suffering. Because we are not gods, it is sometimes easy to use these differences further to divide ourselves from each other. It eases the burden of unconditionally loving all that lives and dies. Do not be mistaken, there is an unbreakable interconnection between all humans, as there is between everything.

We humbly express our thanks to Isabella Virginia Pratt, God, our families and friends from afar and nearby in this magical place that we call home—Holmes County, Ohio. God bless you all.

Grieving

No matter what we believe about the continuation of life after death, for a while at least it does not take away the pain of knowing that we shall not see the person who has died, except in our dreams or in our subtle vision. We most likely shall not be able to hold them, or be held by them; our conversations will be one-sided, and we shall not be doing things together in the way we did before. Earthly contact is gone for a while, and its loss is felt so deeply that the pain a person can experience may even be physical. We may have every outward faith in the fact that our loved one is still 'alive', even more 'alive' than we can imagine. We may 'know', in a manner which is hard to explain, that we will be together again in even more satisfying ways than we had been before, at some point in the future. But, as at any parting, we do miss the person very much indeed.

Thus grief is a natural, earthly feeling to have, and all those who have worked with the bereaved agree that to deny or try to avoid the pain of grief prolongs its effects, and can be detrimental to health.

When looking at the subject of grieving, it can be helpful to approach it from the perspective of being bereaved ourselves, as well as being a friend to someone who is bereaved. Ask the question, 'How can I best serve them so that they are able to grieve in constructive and healthy ways?'. Let us begin with our own needs when we are bereaved, and see how that awareness helps us then to help others.

What do you most need, both as an earthly being, and as a soul, when you are grieving? It might be that you need to be accepted for whatever you are going through, and to know that there are people around who you will listen to you cry, rage, silently weep, mourn, talk, or reminisce. It is good, you will probably agree, to be with people with whom you can share your pain without feeling judged, and without being told what you should and should not do. You might want reassurance that you are not going out of your mind, and that all your difficult and traumatic feelings are usual. At the same time, it is helpful to be near people who can reassure you of the continuance of everyday life. Better still—but this may be a tall order—they would be people who can remind you of the continuation of life eternally, through their own absolute faith and their inner awareness of it. Or it might come from their own experience of coming through the immediate pain of bereavement to a place of certainty that the loss is not permanent. That, of course, is what this book, and the White Eagle teaching it contains, seeks to do: but you may have friends, companions in your worship or counsellors who can provide it too.

So, seek out, if you can, someone who can hold the light for you when you find your arms or heart too weak with sorrow to do so. You may need someone who can cut through the isolation which bereavement can bring, and help you to feel in touch with life again. If this is true for you, my suggestion would be to ask for the specific kind of help you need from someone you know and trust, and to take the prayer for such help into your meditations. We are assured by White Eagle that such a prayer will always be answered—the comfort will come.

Coming to terms with grief—Maureen

My son, Wayne, at the age of thirty-six, died very tragically and suddenly on Wednesday November 1st, 1998, as a result of a motor accident. I tell you this straight out and think you will understand that at the time I was so overcome with grief that I could not think straight and did not know how I was going to go on living a normal life. However, I knew that the Father–Mother God was very much with me and that the prayers of my family and friends sustained me and kept me going.

I immediately contacted Maybelle, our White Eagle group leader here in South Africa, and requested her to come up to Johannesburg from Cape Town to conduct the service for my son. Without hesitation she agreed to come, and from the time she arrived my daughters and I felt her quiet strength.

Wayne had been killed on impact, and that night before I fell asleep I was very aware of his presence in my room. It felt to me as though he was in a panicked state and he did not know what had happened to him, nor where he was. I immediately sat up and explained to him that he had died on the earth plane and that he was now living in another dimension. I told him to walk towards the Light, to follow his angel and his guides and my mother. I said that they would show him the way and look after him. I assured him of my very deep and abiding love and I told him that I was very proud of him and of all that he had achieved on earth. I felt a very loving touch on my brow and I felt his love embrace me. With that he was gone and a very peaceful feeling encompassed me.

The next morning I awoke early and sat in meditation, thinking to myself that I would probably not get through those days as I was far too choked with emotion. Well, this is where the miracle starts. In my meditation those everlasting arms were waiting for me, and without much ado I found myself in the presence of the Father–Mother God, Jesus, White Eagle and the Elder Brethren in the beyond. I am completely unable to describe the overwhelming feeling of love and peace that enfolded me as they stood around me, and it was with the greatest awe and reverence I beheld what was being shown to me. I saw that at the moment of my son's earthly death my mother was waiting to receive Wayne into her arms as a newborn baby. She gazed at me with such love and understanding that it is quite impossible for me ever to forget that look. I just stood and gazed for a long time, and then I thanked everyone for the great honour that had been bestowed on me. I will hold that wondrous happening in my heart and mind forever.

On a lighter note, I would like to tell you that when Wayne was doing his National Service, no matter where he found himself, even in the desert of what was then South-West Africa, he managed to phone home. He was in constant touch with me, and when he could not phone, he stayed in touch with me telepathically. So I always knew that he was alright, even during the time he was fighting a war. Well, nothing daunts Wayne, he has been at it again! One morning after meditation, I was watering the beautiful bouquets which were sent to us at the time of his passing. I turned away from some roses and I got such an overpowering smell of roses that I went back to smell them. Just one rose was absolutely reeking with scent. I looked up and said, 'Hello, Wayne'. He often comes to me during the day or night and he wafts his aftershave at me! I was talking to a friend one evening on the cellphone and it suddenly went dead and Wayne's name appeared on the face of the cellphone.

But the experience that really astounded me was this. I dried two roses from the wreath which was on his coffin and I have placed them very high up on my bookcase, which is in an alcove and does not get any draughts on it. One night I was in bed and those roses landed on the floor with a loud smack. I jumped out of bed because I was sure that they had been damaged; but no, they weren't even slightly damaged, and I knew that Wayne wanted to talk to me. I lit my candle and sat down to meditate. Yes, there was something very specific he wanted me to know and I am sure that I have carried out his particular wishes. I talk to him constantly and I feel his presence very often. That does not mean that I don't miss his physical presence. I do very much, and I know that I will do so for the rest of my life.

Communion garden at New Lands, from a painting by Jennifer Toombs

IX: THE COMFORTER

Although grieving is a natural part of the human process of coming to terms with death White Eagle is quite clear that once we begin to become spiritually aware, something will happen to our consciousness which will help us begin to transcend this pain. Through his teaching he offers us a glimpse of how this can be even with our present limited understanding. Besides helping us know that we are not alone in our grief, he helps us understand that those who have passed on are also still with us, if we would only open our hearts and minds to them. We do not have to stop the natural process of grief for the physical body, but at the same time we can begin to find a deeper companionship than we were perhaps aware of while they were alive. More even than this, there is a spiritual comfort which can come to us which is beyond even our contact with them, though at the time it seems hardly possible. What he begs us not to do is to become bitter in our grief, which cuts us off from the very comfort we need. He says:

We know, dear brethren, we know perhaps even more than you think, just how sorrowful you can be when a loved one is taken from your side, either by death of the physical body, or by misunderstanding. We know how bitter thoughts can creep in when the human emotions are very stirred up, so that you can only feel the bitterness of your own disappointment and grief. Everything around you looks black, and all life seems to be fading away from you because you are cut off from the source of spiritual comfort, from love. Love is God, and when you have no love in your heart because you are bitter through grief or disappointment or misunderstanding, you do not know which way to turn. Then life is black indeed.

When the disciples were feeling completely isolated after Jesus' death, they were told to go to Jerusalem, which means to a higher state of consciousness, and wait for the coming of their Comforter.* The Comforter will come if you will aspire in consciousness to that upper room, which means the higher level of life. In your thoughts rise to that upper room and wait patiently and humbly in communion (that is, in love) with God. Then will come the outpouring of the spirit, the Comforter, even the spirit of truth. When the spirit of truth comes into your soul and heart you are comforted. If you would get love, then give love, and you will be comforted.

If you take the time to attune yourself daily (even if only for five minutes, either in the morning on waking, or at night before going to sleep); if you send out your thoughts to the divine spirit of love, then the Comforter will surely enter your heart, will enter the heart of every one of you. You will know the meaning of the word 'comfort', and you will know what the Comforter is. You will not get this from any other person; although your closest friend or relative, who may be in harmony with you, can help you to be receptive. Each individual must make their own effort, though, and will then know with that inner knowing that this beloved, divine Comforter is waiting to come. The realization may come through a flash of illumination, a flash perhaps in the silence of your own heart. Then you will know the truth about God and the great almighty Spirit, which is the ruler over all life—ruling over all manifestations of life, both on earth and beyond the earth.

Those of you who have lost relatives and friends: be comforted, but more than this, we beg you to endeavour to understand. We ask you to know that there is within you the power

*For the Comforter and what this name siginifies, see the section in chapter I, 'What the Master taught us', and the footnote there to St John's Gospel.

and the means to get in touch with those who have passed away from the darkness of earth. Material thinking brings down the shutter before your vision, but a spiritual quickening, through your worship and love, brings a power superior to anything you can yet understand.

Many have experienced the truth of this message of the living God, for it is when the soul is bereft of a loved one that it is raised above the conditions of mortal life. The soul on earth longs for contact with the one which has gone from the body. Because of this urgent need for a spiritual comforter, the man or woman is raised in consciousness above all earthly things and finds him or herself alone and in the stillness. Then a great love wells up in the human heart: a simple, human love. This is the magnet which attracts the great light of heaven, and the light in the soul of the one who is bereft bursts forth so that the mind and the brain are illumined. The Comforter enters the heart.

*

When you have lost a loved one, recognize that it is only the physical body, like an outworn coat that has lost its usefulness, that you are missing. Hold fast to the truth that spirit is eternal, and that the personality, the beloved personality, is always there. Life changes, the scenes of life change; but the basic, the essential life of a person, the nature of the individual, is eternal. You have also been given the qualities within yourself, and the power, the gifts of the psyche, which enable you to make contact with spirit at will, and with the spirit of your loved ones. What you think habitually you become. If you habitually think along the lines of goodwill, of good thought, God-thought, you draw nearer and nearer every day to your companions who dwell in the light.

They bless you, they love you, and they want you to know that life for them has not ceased, but they continue to live in a happier and freer condition. If you could only be there in that garden of reunion and remembrance you would know that there is no death. The separation is one which you, with your material minds, create. Your dear one is close beside you now.

These dear ones, who are with you, are also living in that state of harmony which you call heaven, because they have heard the voice of goodness, of God. We wish you could see the happiness with which these people work in their own particular section in the spirit world. Each one is drawn, as by a magnet, to the very sphere and to the particular work that their soul most enjoys. Whatever the interest of your loved one, that interest is given to them in their life in spirit. Your loved ones are happy, and they rejoice in their service. They come close to you and they whisper in your heart. Or, if you are trained in meditation and are able to release yourself from the burden and the darkness of your earthly mind—so that you are able to enter the garden of remembrance in the spirit world—then your loved ones immediately come to you. It is the spiritual law of attraction. They come to you if you can imagine with your higher vision that you are with them. It is these inner powers and qualities of the spirit which you have to develop—so that you are always aware, conscious, of the companionship of your loved ones; because in spirit there is no separation.

*

Perhaps a loved one has passed away. All the bereaved has left is a corpse—nothing more. You know, my friends, the agony this brings? But is it true separation? Only for those living in the mortal mind, in the material self. The arisen soul has gone forward into the light—to a state which the mourner, the one who is left behind, can also reach if he or she would rise above the limitations of personal grief. For such grief, my friends, is selfish. We explain that word as meaning limited, of the self only. You say it is natural? Yes, it is of the nature of the earthly self, not the nature of the arisen Christ—which means the arisen Christ in the individual.

When the Christ within can rise and overcome part of the lower personality, then there can be no grief, for there is no separation in spirit. If the bereaved would cast aside his or her limitations and make a supreme effort to rise and meet his or her beloved, he–she would know then that there is no death and no separation.

We should like to say this, particularly to those of you who are bereaved: that in every case release has been the most beautiful experience for each of those individuals. It has been as easy as sleeping and awakening into the eternal and infinite garden and to life in the spirit world. Never, never grieve when your loved one casts aside an old outworn body. Be thankful, *be thankful*: it is a time for thankfulness. Be thankful for the love and the life which you have enjoyed with them. More than this, be thankful for their release into a world of indescribable beauty and peace, happiness and fresh opportunity. Never forget that all around you are these radiant ones, the brothers and sisters of the light, and your own loved ones, who are so close to you in spirit. And you will say, 'Why can't I see them if they are so close?'. You *can* see them, and if the time hasn't arrived yet when you see them, you *will* see them. More than this, you will feel their presence, you will hear their voice, you will hear in your heart what they wish to say to you, what they are endeavouring to convey to you. You yourself must roll away that stone from the tomb.

You have only to think of your loved one to bring them close: not careworn, not suffering; don't think of the pain and the distortion of the countenance during years of suffering. Think of your loved one with a face—with a face like a shining Master,

like Jesus or like Buddha, or any one of the great teachers. Think
of them in that world of light. And remember that when you
are there in meditation, or maybe in a dream, you will notice
how happy they look. How smooth and beautiful then is the face
of your loved one, showing quite clearly the feelings which are
peaceful, joyous and thankful!

*

When the individual first awakens in our world of spirit, after
passing through a stage of disentanglement from earthly values,
that soul cries out for light—more light, more truth—and it
commences to grow, a little more than it was able to grow when
on earth.

The expansion of the spirit within the soul body is like a child
going through the various stages from babyhood to childhood
and adolescence and youth, and then to adulthood and so forth,
in the spirit. You will then ask what is the purpose of reincarnation? Every time the soul reincarnates it brings with it more
spiritual development. It has reached a higher level, and can take
a better place in the school of life. So the soul goes on and on,
with the growth and development of the individuality. Not the
personality, which is different, but the individuality of that tiny
spark of the Great Spirit—until you come into the full glory of
the supreme life of God. Beyond that you cannot think. But think
of life not only as a circle, but as a spiral, round and round and
round, and up and up and up. Do not, therefore, be despondent,
dear earthly brethren: do not be despondent with life.

You are evolving through the different levels of consciousness,
and as you pass onwards and upwards you are assisted by the
very experiences which you cannot understand. The grief of
separation, of losing loved ones, the grief of witnessing death,
the grief of witnessing chaotic conditions on your earth, actually

help you. But you can assist your sister and your brother in their climb towards the mountaintop by your attitude of mind and your thought, your tolerance, your tolerance with all conditions and with all people.

There is a little light inside you, a voice, an urge. Follow it, follow it, dear brethren, and it will lead you to a place of great beauty where your view is expanded. In this place you can really enjoy the blessing of that undoubted love of the great Master who has within his heart you and all your loved ones. It is for you in yourself, by your thoughts, by your aspirations, to reach that level on the mountain where you know there is no separation in life. And then you know you cannot injure or hurt your brother or sister, whoever or wherever he or she is on the path of evolution, without yourself being the injured one. When you injure another, you yourself suffer in the result.

So it is so simple, the key is so simple; and as the ancients said, the key hangs in your heart. If you wish to unlock the door of paradise, of happiness, of beauty in the world of spirit, the key lies within you. It is simply love. Love one another, love life, love your Creator. And know within you that the one you love is as close to you now as ever: closer than ever. The one you love comes to you so clearly. You do not see the physical body, but it may be you can in your memory hear that physical voice, and you know in your heart what that voice is saying to you.

Our resurrection

White Eagle once said,

The bridge which links the physical life to our life in the spirit world is the white ether, the soul substance which you are continually creating within yourself. You are creating and building your soul body out of this white ether, and the white ether builds the bridge to our world. And it is this etheric bridge that you make; you cross it and we cross it to meet you. The meeting place will prove to be a lovely garden, the infinite and eternal garden of creation. By your belief in this love you help to create your perfect garden of the spirit. You will know by experience when you learn the technique of meditation. You will know that it takes you upward to that beautiful, infinite and eternal garden, where the fruits of life grow on the tree in the centre of the garden, the tree of life eternal.

In the following sections White Eagle continues to explore the nature of the relationship between physical matter and the inner world, and the 'bridge' which we can build and use to pass from one state of consciousness to the other. He begins by showing us how Jesus' resurrection was an example of our own, or of the possibility of our own. He goes on to talk about what the practice of inner contemplation and the creative use of the imagination can do to accustom us to crossing that bridge. If we can learn to do this while in our bodies, then when the time comes to leave them our stepping forward into our eternal home, in our etheric form, will be as natural to us as walking into an earthly garden.

We want you to realize that in your physical body you are clothed in a shell, like the little creatures at the bottom of the sea, but that you can break through that shell by your own effort. There are some people who do not understand that they themselves must make an effort truly to live. Similarly, it takes effort to rise in consciousness into the world of Eternal Life. Remember this, because there has come a time now when there is much controversy on your earth—much controversy one individual with another, one religious sect with another, and one political sect with another. But do remember that in life all are one. *There is no death*. There is continual life. And we would explain to you that your Christian scriptures are telling you of the life eternal. There is no death. And all the great masters are also saviours, because they are bringing to human kind this truth. They are demonstrating by their physical life, they are teaching through a physical body, that there is no death.

Let us turn to the passage in your scriptures where the sorrowful disciples had lost their Lord, their beloved.* They had lost sight of his physical body. Now you have all at some time in your life passed through this deep experience of grief and sorrow, because you have lost the one nearest and dearest to you, someone whom you loved, whom you felt to be part of you. You have lost them because they have changed their form, and the form that they left behind you have seen lying in a casket, in a sepulchre. And where, *where* is your loved one?

You will notice that it was the woman who went to the sepulchre. This is symbolic of the soul of the individual, the soul is the woman. Men have the soul, the woman-principle, within them, as well as those who are physically women.

When you have seen the body of your own beloved lying in its casket, remember the words in the Bible. When Mary called for the Master, *Rabboni,* there he was by her side. Now, from the world of spirit we have frequently seen the grief which is around earth man and woman as they weep over a shell. Yet by their side has been standing, pulsating with light and love, the one for whom they grieved. We suggest to you that when the experience of the change of life from a lower level to a higher level comes to you, above all remember that you cannot die. You, the real you, the true you, the love which you feel, the sympathy which you feel, the kindness which you feel for all creatures both in nature and in the animal kingdom—in the birds of the earth, in the

*Principally, the last chapters of St John's Gospel, nos. XX and XXI, but also in St Luke's Gospel, chapter XXIV, and briefly at the end of Matthew and Mark.

very air itself—all of this is you, and is living in God eternally. Because God is your breath of life. And when you shuffle off the mortal coil you still breathe, but very much more comfortably. You still breathe and pulsate with this heavenly life, which is universal and eternal.

Many, many people, when they leave the physical body, do not know that they have left it. There is apparently no change except that when they speak to their loved one they get no response. Now, do not think you are crazy if you respond to what you imagine your loved one is saying to you after he or she has passed from the physical shell. Remember this: speak to them in your heart, for in your heart is the union, *union* between you and your loved one. This is the truth which the whole world will know and accept when each individual being has learnt to love—unashamedly to love. *Love*, my children, is the most beautiful emotion there is.

You remember the disciples were so excited when they were able to see what they thought was the physical body of Jesus. They thought they were seeing the physical body, but actually they were seeing the etheric body, which is so closely interwoven with the physical one. From the physical the etheric body is created and built up. And Jesus said to them, *Touch me not; for I am not yet ascended to my Father*. Now, this statement puzzles many people, and we are going to give you this explanation.

'Touch me not, I am fragile, I am in a body which is not eternal, but I am going to rise into a celestial body which is eternal, and that can be felt, that can be touched'. St Paul clearly stated that there is a terrestrial body, the physical and the etheric together; and there is a celestial body. When you leave that terrestrial body which is frail and impermanent, you are in your celestial body, which is eternal and infinite. And in that body your consciousness expands, and you become part of the whole of creation. You are not absorbed into it so that you lose your individual consciousness.

That is something which worries many people. 'I do not want to lose my own individuality'. Make your individuality Godlike and you will live eternally in the whole universe, in the flowers, in the springtime, in the sunshine, in the rippling water, in the life in the sea, the life on earth, the life in the sky. You will become at one and feel and understand the feelings, and understand the ever-great evolution. The Father, the Mother, and we are all one, and peace is with us. We are at peace together, together when we attain that level of the celestial spheres of eternal life. This eternal life is with you now. It is within you; but the experiences on the earth are helping you to grow in consciousness and in comprehension of what life is.

*

My friends, there is so much beauty in the human soul, and so much glory in the spirit. For when the spirit is sufficiently developed to take complete possession of the soul, that spirit shines through the man or woman. And when this happens you regard such people as saints. We would not have you limit your saints to the orthodox church. There are countless saints all over the world, not necessarily attached to any organization or religion. They are saints because the love in them causes them to give selfless service to life, service to all creatures and to all human beings. They are saints because the joy of heaven bubbles in them and they want to sing and dance. Jesus danced with joy and sang with joy, the joy of the spirit. And this is the world that your loved ones have entered.

When one of your number passes on, he or she finds a great welcome in our world. All of you have many friends in what you call the afterlife. But do not think of the invisible life as a place or condition that you cannot reach or be aware of while on earth. We come to speak for those who have passed through the veil of so-called death; those who have vanished from your sight for a while, but who are with you now. All around you are shining ones, who are thought by so many to be dead and gone. But, my children, there is no death, only life. All is life, eternal life. Use your imagination at this moment. How would you feel if you left your physical body but hardly realized that you had left it, and you found yourself very close to your loved ones, to your family and your friends—and yet they would not take any notice of you? You speak to them, you touch them, but they take no notice. Remember this image, and remember that within you God has placed the key, the key to a wider and grander and more beautiful life. You are so engaged in this earth world with earthly things, with physical things, with material things, that you have no time, no energy, no will, to think of the world around you, a world which is infinitely more beautiful than anything you can see or touch or hear with your physical senses.

You cannot contact spiritual life with your physical senses, you can only contact spiritual life, the life beyond the grave, with your spiritual senses. The time has come for you to awaken to your spiritual potentialities, to listen with your inner hearing, to use the senses of your celestial body. You are building and developing that spiritual body and the spiritual senses, which are replicas of the earthly senses, with the addition of a sixth sense, which some people call the intuition. This intuition is the inner sense of the spirit within, and the time has come when this inner sense is being developed.

The path before every one is a path of light. The son of God is the light, and he has put into the heart of every man, woman and child a light to guide them on that path which leads to the golden world of reunion and joy. You don't need to die physically to follow that path. All people will learn in time that they can reach that world of light by their own efforts, not when they leave the shell of the physical body, not when they change their garments, but at all times. Whatever they are doing, in the workshop, in the garden, in the home, in the business world, and wherever they are, people can think not only of matter, physical matter, but know also that they are for ever eternally linked, eternally united, with that divine spirit. They are always linked to the Father–Mother from whom they have come. That cord, that cord of light is ever there. Whatever you are doing on earth, just a thought and you are with your heavenly company. They have their own work to do, but their spirit is with you if you think about them—mentally and quietly think of them, give your love and ask their help, and be at peace within.

There are those seeking for conviction, because the hunger of love within urges them to find out where some loved one goes at death. One can obtain proof of the continuity of life after death. Never mind if the seeker only contacts the immediate next world, the lower astral plane. All serves a purpose, and is true; and it is right that communication and proofs should be given to the enquirer. But the deeper students of the mystery schools know that life is continuous. If you know, then the light is born within; you leave behind the search for evidence, which is but an endless repetition—like a gramophone record ever repeating the same thing. The light within says, 'I know; there is no death; my loved one cannot die; she, he, still lives'.

Creating the bridge: attunement to the inner worlds

When someone we love dies, they too create a 'bridge' for us into the inner world. Often people have reported that for some time after the passing, they have felt more attuned to spiritual things than before. The connection of love between two people is, as White Eagle says, like a cord which can never be broken, and as the dying person passes on so they take a part of their loved one with them. Another way to look at it is that the one who dies opens up a doorway as they pass into the light, which remains open for a while for those who would visit.

The time after a loved one dies is therefore a good time for the bereaved person to begin to attune themselves to their loved one in a different way. The more often the consciousness is raised to the next level of life, the more easily this is done, and the temporary 'bridge' becomes more and more stable.

Meditation has already been mentioned as one method of raising our consciousness to the next level of life. Prayer and contemplation, particularly of the natural world, are others, as White Eagle goes on to describe.

You long to have physical contact with your loved ones who have passed onwards. We cannot blame you, for we understand that longing to touch the hand which has gone and to see the vacant chair filled. 'We long to feel their touch', you will say. Yes, we know; we know that longing—but there is an even better way than holding on to the physical body. Remember, a physical body is merely a form of dress, which is something you will fully appreciate when you come to shed your present one. On earth, you feel rather pleased to have some fresh clothes, and when your old ones are tired you send them away. But when it comes to the physical clothing, however old and decrepit it is, you still long to keep it with you.

Now this is a bridge which you have to cross. We do not mean the bridge from our world to your world that we have been speaking about. We do not mean the bridge which you cross at death. We mean a bridge which you cross in full consciousness while you are on earth.

What do we mean by this? We mean that while you are living in a physical body and in a very material world, you have to strive to realize that you are not your body, but that you are a spirit being, clothed for a time in a certain body. When you can look beyond that clothing and that material life, you will see a much finer world, a world which is quite as real and solid as the physical matter, but a world composed of much finer and more sensitive matter.

One way truly to become aware that you are not your body is through constant endeavour to accept that there are other worlds in which you, the son–daughter of God, can live. You are bound by the intellect and your body, but when you turn to the deep holy sanctuary which is within your soul, then you receive a manifestation, a demonstration. It comes not through a physical body, but through a spiritual power which is far more convincing than a physical body. And why? Because in that holy sanctuary a jewel resides: Christ, the son of God your Creator.

When you contact that spirit power you are convinced—you know—that you are an eternal being, and that all of the human race are eternal beings too. You know that there is a state of life beyond the present house of flesh—a world of beauty, of ever-unfolding glory and opportunity. There, those souls who have shed their old dress and have let go their contact and their longing for physical matter, find themselves in a world of beauty and harmony and brotherhood of the spirit. They find that they have companions who understand their innermost needs. They find that these companions will guide them to the exact place where they will find happiness. Not in singing psalms all day, not in lying about doing nothing, but in being engaged in some study or pursuit which is after their own heart—that is where their happiness lies.

As for those who have left the earth through being sacrificed in a war, something which has come about through the ignorance of the world, they find a particular comfort and happiness in our world. Sacrifice of the individual, self-sacrifice, brings great blessing to the soul. It wipes out so much of what you would call 'sin'. No-one innocently suffers, because the so-called innocent sufferers are gathered into the great arms of love. These conditions of war that come to the earth plane, although they are brought about by ignorance and stupidity, are turned to good effect. No-one is sacrificed in vain, and with war there comes a corresponding push forward in the evolution of humanity. All the time spiritual growth continues in you, and not only spiritual growth, but mental growth. Better conditions of life are the result of past suffering.

We see the wonderful growth which has taken place in the world over quite a few years, and we see stirring in the mind and soul some awareness of spiritual development, just a little awareness. This awareness of invisible things is coming: knowledge that things are not what they seem; that behind all life is thought and imagination. If you had no imagination you would be no more than clods! You must have imagination before there is creation. In creating the earth God held in His–Her mind the whole of creation. No-one can move outside the circle of God's thought. Humanity is held in the love of God.

Do not be afraid of your imagination

Imagination, which is so little understood, is the doorway into our world—into the higher ethers, the higher and finer etheric world. The key which unlocks that door is hanging in your heart. It is through love, love of God, love of all that is good. Truth, wisdom, light, beauty are the key which unlocks the door of imagination, which takes you into that world of spirit.

We are not limited and bound as you are by the flesh, and we come back to tell you that there is no death, and that your loved ones are very close beside you. Those who can open the door of their imagination will see them. They come to reassure you, to love you and help you to traverse the path of life which will lead you, without fail, into a life of infinite beauty, here, while you are enclosed in a body.

Remember to walk your way through life in the full consciousness that in body and spirit we are one. All people are one. You cannot injure any of God's creatures without injuring yourself. You cannot love and give kindness to any of God's children without receiving love and kindness yourself. This is the message of the at-one-ment.

You must cultivate imagination, not only imagination of places and form, but imagination of feeling. This is what is wrong with humanity at its present stage of evolution. It has no imagination of the effect of its own speech and emotions upon other creatures, including other people. Imagination is the primary quality for you to develop, because it is only through imagination that you learn the feelings of others. And this, my dear ones, is the key to love.

When you have developed your power of imagination so that you can put yourself into the place of other human beings, you can put yourself in the place of all nature, into the place of the animal kingdom and be sensitive to the suffering which can be inflicted on animals by people. When you have developed your power of imagination, when you have developed your sensitivity and your feeling, and when you can feel through your imagination the suffering and pain of other people, then you are developing that true love, the power of love.

Someone asked us once what our world is like. We will give you a picture of the spirit world, for there is so much confusion when you are told that the world we come from is a mental world. It is true that it is a mental world insofar as it is composed of thought. Let us explain it to you in this way, that when you develop your power of imagination and the power of love which all these other things promote and stimulate, you will find that in your meditations you will see beautiful things, and not ugly things. You will see the world of God. That world is governed by love.

The more you develop this sensitivity to the needs and the feelings of your companions, the more you are developing your vision and your hearing and your appreciation of beauty. You are developing your soul qualities. So when you no longer have a physical body, when you just get up and leave it lying down there, you will have no more interest in it, and you will find yourself in a spirit state of life.

You cannot resuscitate that physical body, but you want a body of some kind. You want senses to enable you to move around and see where you are. Unless you have developed those senses in your earth life by being kind and loving, by appreciating the glory of nature, the beauty of flowers and trees, the joy of the song of birds, the glory of the sunrise and the sunset; unless you have developed an appreciation of God's gifts in your own being, that is the gift of hearing sound, beautiful sounds, and of seeing beautiful things on the earth plane, you will be quite a long time in the spirit world before you can actually see and feel its glory. But one day at last you will be able to say: 'Oh, I am happy! God is everywhere around me. I know the meaning of joy, I know the meaning of happiness, and I am free'.

There can be no death, only creation and dissolution, coming together again in creation, and so on throughout the rhythm of life. When you have reached to the centre of the truth which is God, spirit, you will be only conscious of eternally living and will not be separated at any time from those you love. Some people will call that level of consciousness that you can touch cosmic consciousness.

If you who are reading our words have lost dear ones by the falling away of the physical body, the release of the spirit—if you have lost the physical form—then we advise you to use your thought power and see your loved ones. Think of them, speak to them, spirit to spirit. This takes a little time for you to understand, but if you persevere in your quiet moments thinking of the spirit world as a world of eternity—always there, always being brought into the vision, into manifestation—you will eventually live in that consciousness of life. You will be aware of life not in all its drabness and suffering and restriction in a physical body, but aware of a life which is free like the lark in the sky.

When we are bereaved, we long for some contact with our loved one, and it is often the most ordinary contact which we crave—just to see them walk in the door from the garden or from work; to see them sitting at the table eating, or watching their favourite game on television. In previous teaching, White Eagle has described how very much like the earth heaven can be, and how, in that state, our loved one can seem just as he or she was on earth. In the passage that follows he is asking us not to limit ourselves by how we long to see our loved one. It is difficult for someone on the other side of death to contact those on earth, because of the limits of space and time, and the difference in their state of consciousness. To us, those in spirit often appear as beings of light, and their contact with us can be very subtle. It is their etheric body which we perceive in some way, and this is lighter, gentler in vibration on all levels. Moreover, it is our etheric senses which, consciously or unconsciously, we are using, and they will register impressions which are not so earthy as we are used to, but more ethereal and ephemeral. To explain this, White Eagle recounts an experience that he had.

We want to tell you a little story. A bereaved wife was talking to us on one occasion. 'Oh White Eagle', she said, 'I do not want to see my dear husband in all his spirit robes. I want to see him in his tweeds, wielding his golf club, then I shall be happy'. How well we understand this feeling, but if only she could have taken her eyes above the old tweeds and golf club, she would have seen the real person she loved! Maybe she wouldn't see him in the clothing of earth, but in shining raiment which is the real spirit, the real person she loved. You too, if you are bereaved, may feel the gentle presence of your loved one. It may be like a beautiful breeze. You may feel the gentle touch on face or hand or arm, and you may brush it aside and say, 'It is my imagination'. Do not be too sure. Keep your balance, certainly. Be wise and balanced, but be receptive to the heavenly breeze, the heavenly light, the white garment, the gentle touch, the sweet music of the heavens. You don't want to drag that dear beloved one back into the density and the heaviness of a dark earth. You are really happy that he or she is alive and free and can meet you clearly in that heavenly garden.

When you join your loved one in spirit, remember that it is only on earth that there is a passage of time. When you leave your body you will meet your loved ones exactly as you were, and they were, when the physical separation came. When that reunion comes it will be as though loss had never been. May this comfort you, and help you in your need today.

X. AWAKENING ON THE OTHER SIDE OF LIFE: ARE WE DIFFERENT?

UNDERSTANDABLY, there are anxieties in many people's minds about what they may find when they arrive at the next level of consciousness after death, and about what is happening to those they love who are already there. Historically, world religions and literature are full of stories about purgatory and judgment, some of which are very frightening. White Eagle gives us an infinitely more beautiful picture of what actually happens. It should be understood in the context of the rest of his teaching about the wise and loving spirit in which we all are held, and which resides in us all. There may be some readers to whom it seems so wonderful and so far-reaching as to be beyond our grasp? If this thought arises, consider this reassuring statement he has made elsewhere: 'We tell you, my dear ones, that *if you can put into practice in your daily life one iota of what you hear flowing through from us in words, you will do very well indeed*'.

Many of us live with the fear that we are not good enough. We may understand the need to be loving and kind. We may see our defensiveness producing negative results. We may long to feel free from the trivial dislikes and pettiness of the earthly personality, but we may feel that the struggle is too much for us. This effort, even the weariness that goes with it, is part of our learning and part of entering into life in fullness, so that spontaneously we may one day act wholly out of love in all circumstances. This is White Eagle's teaching. But we are not at that stage yet, and no-one understands more than he, and those in spirit who have been through the same process, the need for patience and for forgiveness of this limited earthly self.

On awakening

Immediately a soul is released from the physical body and comes to our world, it starts a process of awakening. This may seem to you to contradict what you have learnt, because undoubtedly, as you measure time, a period elapses for many souls before they awaken to the consciousness of their new life. But remember that in the world of spirit there is no consciousness of time. Thus a soul may apparently wake up immediately after death—and yet by your measurement of time its period of quiescence may have been longer. This 'length of time' is conditioned by the state of the man or woman at the time of passing on; but usually the one who has been interested in spiritual truth quickly awakens to his or her surroundings in the spirit life.

As soon as he or she is able to become consciously active, the soul lessons start. This is even though the person is no more aware that he or she is learning lessons than the average man or woman on your earth is aware that he or she is learning, and so gradually evolving his or her spiritual aspect. One of the most usual methods of teaching a soul is to take it to the Hall of Records, where it reviews all the episodes in its life. Nothing is said to the soul; it just sees itself as it truly is. Strength and courage are necessary to look into the mirror and to see yourself reflected, without camouflage; but accompanying this experience comes the teacher, in the guise of an acceptable friend, who encourages and helps the one who is learning, in a most gentle and beautiful way. The teacher neither condemns nor chides, but helps the pupil to understand and to learn that every life on earth is the result of former experiences. You see, everything in the world of spirit is under the divine law of love.

You are your own judge and your own punisher. The suffering you endure on earth and in spirit is self-inflicted, though you do not realize it. Even on earth if you do something that you know is foolish, some repercussion demonstrates to you how foolish you have been. You see, spiritual growth is all based upon the law of sowing and reaping, and yet we would impress upon you the gentleness and love which governs the operation of this law.

Truths that are revealed to your spirit have to be translated to the earth life. When you are able to go into the centre of your being, into the very heart of creation, into the centre of life, to the place of quiet and stillness of mind, emotions and body, then deep within the centre of your being you realize the true way to act, to live.

We who come from that inner world are well aware of the practical details of human life. You may think that we, being spirit, are quite remote from the activities and the pains and the fears and the sufferings of our brother or sister on earth. Here you would be very much mistaken. The brotherhood in the world of spirit, they of the White Light, are closely concerned with the evolution, happiness and wellbeing of all human kind. We have passed through many incarnations and have the means of recalling these human experiences when necessary. Therefore we can feel with you; we can understand your frustrations, your limitations and your anxieties and fears. We can understand physical pain and spiritual suffering. We are part of you; we are one of you; we are with you, all of you. But we love you; therefore we do not remove your problems and difficulties, for this would be neither kind nor good for you. We can only stand by your side and give you our strength and love, while you slowly learn by trial and error.

As a result of your dealing with these difficulties, if you are moving on the clear path of light and are open to the message being brought to you from the spirit, you will receive into your souls joy which would be lost to you if we were to remove your problems and difficulties. Only you, in companionship with the God working in your heart, can experience the heavenly joy of learning those necessary truths. Each time your eyes are opened

to the right way of life, each time you are able to touch the secret level of life, the light expands in your heart and soul, and
life takes on a new aspect. You see, with eyes both spiritual and
physical, a lovelier vista, a more profound beauty than you have
seen before; and your heart will sing with praise and thanksgiving to your Creator.

Let us give you a simple example of what we mean. It is said
that a young woman and man truly in love see the world as
something so much more beautiful than they did before. Love
has quickened the spirit within them, and love, even in its lowliest
form, still has a magical power. It makes the lovers happy and
reveals beauty to them. What we are trying to tell you is just the
same. It is through life's simple everyday experiences that you
must find your way to God and truth.

We are trying, brethren, to bring you right into the innermost
centre of life and into your own innermost centre, which is the
basis of all action and the centre from which you will receive an
answer to every problem. From that centre, pulses of life go out
throughout the universe. These pulsations, these forces, some
of which are called positive and others negative, permeate all
things. Now you are already a sensitive instrument and through
spiritual development and unfoldment you are training yourself
to react to these forces in a correct and balanced way, not allow-
ing yourself to be pulled too much one way or another. You are
learning to keep on a steady path of light; to become perfectly-
balanced souls. A master is a perfectly-balanced soul, one who
reacts in the right and balanced way to all the influences which
play upon him or her.

All men and women are linked, consciously or unconsciously,
with the Supreme Power, God, and this is why they have the urge
to pray for help from an unknown source, a higher power. It is
natural even from childhood for people to reach out to something

they can love and believe in and respect. When the child grows older, even if it has become what you may call a materialist, there are times of crisis when it instinctively calls out to God.

Over all human life a guiding power is watching at all times. But it rests with you yourself whether you will act in accordance with that guidance or whether, on the other hand, you will turn your face away; whether you will act foolishly and go over to the darkness—or, in old-fashioned language, Satan. But Satan is only another word for Saturn, the tester; and even the negative force is slowly and painfully working in life to test and purify you and all humanity, and eventually bring you wisdom, bring you light.

You are in the human body for a twofold purpose. First, you are here to learn to find the glory of God, both in yourself and in all life. Second, you have to discover through incarnation those spiritual truths through which you will achieve infinite happiness. The law is that each human being shall love God with heart and soul and mind.* In doing so he or she naturally learns to love his or her neighbour, because that neighbour is God, and God is in the neighbour. You see, we are all of us coming gradually to the realization that life is all one grand whole. You cannot become isolated from God or your neighbour. The tendency in all life is towards unification. First, we repeat, come the development and the growth of the individual and the God-consciousness in the individual, and then the unification in full consciousness with the whole of life. You know then that you cannot hurt any living thing without hurting yourself, the whole of life; and that every tear you dry, every pain your remove from your brother–sister, comes back to you in blessing.

The soul is also linked to planetary and zodiacal influences. Hence the incoming soul makes its own choice of birth. Many

*The reference throughout this paragraph is Matthew 22 : 37–39

find the science of astrology difficult to accept, because it seems to indicate that destiny outweighs freewill. But there is no accidental birth: in fact birth is the result of a divine law controlling and guiding the evolution of every soul.

We would not paint too sombre a picture of the soul world, but a clear one. Remember that *nothing* is attained in any life without work, without effort. Many think that to go through life carelessly, and without thought, so long as they are reasonably 'decent', will ensure them a heaven. Kindliness and love are two attributes which draw to the soul the more beautiful substance; and therefore if that soul body is sensitive, beautiful, refined in texture, it will necessarily vibrate and respond to beauty which it alone can appreciate. If the soul substance is coarse, it cannot react to the beauty of the higher degrees of the soul life. Should the physical body live on earth in love instead of cruelty, in kindliness instead of hate, in refinement instead of crudity, then this same physical body helps to evolve the soul body, and contributes to the soul substance through the emotions and desires.

We want to describe to you the true state of life after the soul has passed through what some people call the purgatorial spheres. By the purgatorial spheres we mean that state of mind in which the soul finds itself when it has long been bound by selfish desires. After death each soul will have gradually to work through these desires. Then it is able to rise into a condition of happiness and beauty. While the human spirit is essentially pure and the spirit life pure and beautiful, when the spirit incarnates it becomes entangled with the desires of the flesh. In the beginning of its life in form, the spirit can be likened to a little child, a babe. Its light and power is so dim in both the body and in the soul that you can hardly recognize its existence in the people you contact in the ordinary, everyday world.

Now, the purpose of incarnation after incarnation is actually to force the growth of that spirit into the full consciousness of its relationship to the divine. This full consciousness is only attained by long and varied experience in the body. You may still ask, 'Why need the beautiful spirit descend yet again into such darkness and bondage?'. We answer that only through continued contact with matter can the spirit gain its strength and growth. A child may have the potentialities of a great man or a great woman, but has yet to grow towards that finished form. So also with the spirit. When you find life particularly hard and limiting, remember that the purpose of that limitation is to teach you to rely upon the power of the divine Son within. Most people prefer to rely upon material things, upon money, mental equipment and their own ability to do things well. They go off that path which the spirit would take. But when there comes a call upon that inner strength, upon the inner Son of God, then progress is made and real growth takes place.

When the soul at last comes to the end of an incarnation, it passes onward. And when all dross has been consumed, the soul goes forward into one of the upper astral planes, or into a world of light somewhat similar to the earthly plane. The same forms of scenery are there, such as mountains and rivers, woods and gardens, flowers and trees, and there are nature spirits—fairies, elves, gnomes and sprites—that abound in the astral world. Its people live in a state of intense happiness. Everything about them is as perfect as can be. They could not have reached that state, that spirit plane we are describing, if they could not appreciate the perfection of that life.

We will explain what we mean. When the soul leaves its body it has to pass through this intermediary stage. If its consciousness of that spiritual life has been awakened on the earth, it will traverse that intermediary place in a sleeping state and awake in the heaven world. If, on the other hand, there has been little development spiritually, the soul may find itself like a horse wearing blinkers, unable to see the glorious country in which it is living. This is where the importance of meditation comes in. Once you are awakened, you will commence to use your imagination and your powers of meditation. By exercise of these powers you will find yourself in beautiful places. You will see grand scenery, lovely snowcapped and sunlit mountains, beautiful valleys and rivers. You will see rainbow colours in everything, and you may see the most perfect architecture and wonderful temples. All these things you people say exist only in your imagination. Not wholly; they are actually places that you see when your spirit is released, for then you penetrate that world of light; even if only in vision, you see into the higher world.

A mirror of light

All are servants of the whole. A craftsperson is a servant, a builder is a servant, a writer is a servant. Those who act or play on a stage for the pleasure and enjoyment of other people are all servants. And we want to bring this point home to you. Whatever your calling in life—whether you are a farmer, an artist, or a writer, or whether you follow any one of the professions—you are all servants of other beings. And as servants the God within you is teaching you to be good servants: to be a good hairdresser, to be a good manager, to be a good gardener, to be a good farmer.

Now this you will find demonstrated in the world of Spirit. For when you have slipped off your mortal body, you will immediately find yourself in a world similar to the one you have left. Don't make the mistake of thinking that immediately you leave your earthly body you are an angel with wings—or that you will be great spirits because you have believed in life after death. You will be exactly the same as you are now. And what you love now, which will probably be your home, or your garden, or the land that you are farming, or the work you are doing in an office, those will be the conditions in which you will find yourself. How they feel will depend upon how you have executed your work: whether you have done it earnestly and honestly with a desire to serve, or whether you have done it for a selfish reason to gain and acquire for yourself wealth. You will find that the latter will be as dust and ashes. It will mean nothing to you. But what will bring you love and joy and true happiness will be when you meet your loved ones, those whom you truly love; those whom you have truly served.

Let us take, for example, a mother who loves—or nearly always loves!—her family: loves her husband, her children, her home. If she is blessed with a garden of flowers, she will be in that garden. But, after the mists of earth have rolled away, she will find her vision will become much clearer, and she will find that her garden is her ideal, full of perfect flowers, no weeds. Well now, think what it would be like to have a garden which has no weeds in it! I am sure that all of you who have gardens wish the weeds would not grow: but may we remind you from the so-called weeds evolve very nice flowers?

And what were weeds in your gardens, what were sown as weeds according to your life and your relationship with your sister and brother, and your true worship of God—those weeds will have become most beautiful flowers in this higher world. We can never describe to you the beauty of such gardens in the spirit world as we have seen.

While we are talking of gardens in the spirit world, there is someone here before us who brought a little bouquet of sweet smelling flowers from her father's spirit garden, and they lie here on my desk.* These flowers although they were picked in an

* *White Eagle was talking to a congregation meeting for worship, and referring to the reading desk Grace Cooke was using at the time.*

earthly garden, have the spirit of love, and they are the replica of the flowers which grow in your Father's spirit garden. Now, we are telling you the truth … and we come back to give you comfort. And the age now beginning—the age of Aquarius, the age of brotherhood—is the age when all the world will believe and know that life beyond death is a fact, a truth. It will be proved according to your scientist brethren—who think they know so much at present! But they will change their minds, as they always do; and they will find that yes, life after death, life without a physical body, is the true life, and is eternal life.

When you come to the spirit world, after the preliminary stage of learning, you will find yourself free in a body which is sweet and beautiful and clothed in heavenly raiment. You will find that there are orchards of fruit. Can you imagine living without a body, or being entirely happy without food or without a drink to satisfy your thirst? Of course not! The life in spirit is the same as life on earth, only very much more comfortable and beautiful and satisfying. When you are hungry you just walk into the garden. You will then pick the lovely piece of fruit from the tree, and you will find it most satisfactory. You will not go out and slaughter the animals for your food, you will not go out and catch the poor fish in the waters, or shoot the birds in the air. You will be there in this world of Spirit that is harmonious to you, and beautiful in every possible way.

People often ask, 'What do the people in the spirit life eat? Can they really eat? What do they do there?'. Well, there are perfect and delicious fruits at the astral level. If the spirit desires food, it can pluck from the tree the fruits of the spirit, or indeed any other kind of food that appeals. In higher spheres desire for food fades. Nevertheless, we want you to understand that the spirit world is solid and real, and those who live there can as easily banquet if they want to. They can eat very delicious food and drink a liquid which is somewhat like your wine, but is actually a spiritual substance. But then all food and fruits are spiritual in essence there, because they are on a spiritual plane of life. They are, however, just as real to us as your coarse foods are to you. Those who dwell on higher spheres can clothe themselves as they wish in most beautiful soft materials, such as do not exist on earth. What we are trying to tell you is that in the spirit world life is as 'real' as on your earth, only infinitely more beautiful.

Another question arises sometimes. 'Do you grow old in the spirit world? Why is it sometimes that we see a spirit man or a woman who appears to be old?'. Well, there is no age in the astral world, only a period of maturity. A person may appear mature but never decrepit, always full of life, health and wellbeing. A spirit can clothe itself at will, and often will visit the earth wearing the appearance of the body it wore at the end of its last incarnation. It will appear like that in order to be recognized, but on return to the astral plane it is again at the perfection of manhood or womanhood. You like to have a change of dress? We, too, have a wardrobe containing different dresses that we can adopt at will. For instance, we may clothe ourselves with a typical white robe and a turban. We may clothe ourselves as an inhabitant of Atlantis, with a crown of feathers like the plumed serpent. We may be seen sometimes as a Native American, with a crown of eagle's feathers. Some of my brethren from that incarnation are very proud of their feathers, because every feather has been won. The wearer has gone through some grave ordeal to win each feather in their crown or headdress.

We may at will adopt the dress of our incarnation as an Egyptian priest. You also will do the same. Whatever you have been, whatever incarnation you have had, you always have the right to adopt that dress. It is yours. You have grown into it and the clothing belongs to you. Of course, incarnations with which the soul is not very pleased can fade right away and disintegrate, if the soul prefers.

There are beautiful palaces and buildings in the world of spirit, such as great laboratories for the use of the scientists, and very wonderful observatories for the astronomers. There are beautiful art galleries and music rooms, halls for music lovers, and gardens of exquisite beauty for gardeners. Every conceivable desire is supplied in the world beyond this. Beyond and beyond and beyond—there is no limitation to the life of the spirit. We could go on talking for a long time about this life beyond the earth. You see, the earth has an astral world all around it that is far more beautiful and radiant than itself. There are many planets in the heavens that are purely astral and not composed of earth matter as you understand it. These luminous bodies exist in the heaven spheres when the soul, having undergone crucifixion, finds eternal life, such as was demonstrated by the master Jesus. Afterwards that soul has power to create or to materialize a body at will, which can travel through space or to any sphere of life it desires.

The inner consciousness

There are temples and lodges and recognizable places in the ether. The white ether, we would tell you, is more solid and more real than your physical environment, for in it lies the record of eternal life. The physical state is transient; it is not as real as it seems; the nature of physical matter is change, change, change. The state of white ether is growth, growth, growth, moulding itself by the will of the divine Creator into infinite eternal beauty.

You can comprehend neither infinity nor eternity. It is useless for us to try to describe them because it is impossible to comprehend infinity with a finite brain and mind. Nonetheless, you can listen when we tell you that deep, deep within you, in the inner planes of consciousness, are worlds of indescribable and unbelievable perfection. You can hear when we say that as you learn to command yourself, your emotions, your fears, your anxieties—as you learn to enter into the sanctuary of peace in preparation—you will by your own freewill and power advance into the glories of a world perfect in form, colour, harmony. It will be a world of music, a world of goodness, a world where everything falls into its appointed place without hindrance.

When you have learned, through meditation, prayer and aspiration, to hold inner communion with the heaven world, you will start to see the luminosity of that world, the beauty of it. As you gaze into the world beyond, into our world of spirit, you will see that all forms are luminous. They all look as though they have their own light within them, so that nature, the very trees, instead of looking solid, will look as if they have a light inside them.

All nature looks like this, and all the people look like this. This is also how you will know that you have true vision, when you can see the difference between a thought form and the true spirit. The true spirit is illumined, and is radiating light.

The world of spirit is beautiful, and to this world every created thing passes. You will all live in that world of light, of luminosity. To put it into the words of a man who passed on into our world of spirit: he wanted to comfort his wife and to tell her about the new life that he was in. She asked him, 'Well, what is it like? What is your body like? What are your clothes like?'. And his reply was, 'My dear, my body is all light, and I am clothed with light'. Imagine what this means. Imagine seeing those in spirit, seeing your own parents, or family, in spirit. You will see them illumined—all light—looking so happy and so beautiful, because they have been removed from the mists and the darkness and heaviness of physical matter.

How are they living now?

Most of your friends and dear ones who have gone on are still living in much the same way as formerly, because there are many similar interests available in the spirit world—many activities. The young can still enjoy their games; the young people who like cars or enjoyed flying can still operate them if they continue to want to. You see life in the spirit world can be a replica of life as lived on the physical plane. The bodies which are used there, although created out of soul matter, or the higher ether, are replicas of the physical body, and seem just as solid to them as the physical body appeared.

Life in the spirit world is close by, and interpenetrates your mortal life. Your memory plays a great part in increasing the happiness of those who have passed on. When you remember them, when you think of them thankfully and joyfully, and when you are imagining them as you knew them, enjoying health, vigour and happiness, that memory goes to them instantly, and they know then that you are with them. They know that there is no distance, no separation between you. They are closer to you than breathing; right inside your soul they are with you.

Proof of this continued life is being given all the time, although many shut it out by saying, 'Yes, I did think about my old friend. I even imagined that he came back to see me. But of course it was all nonsense, and I put the idea aside'. Nevertheless, these impressions that are received are true.

You wonder what your relatives and friends who have gone on now do? They are not sitting on a cloud playing a harp, although the harp is a wonderful instrument. It has a sound which is creative and has power over the ether. In other words, it builds. Your friends are not continually playing harps, but they are sounding the keynote, the sound of the etheric kingdom, and they are studying according to their aspirations.

You know when you have done your best with your school studies that it does not end there. You find that those were elementary. The same law applies to your spiritual studies. When you apply yourself earnestly and sincerely to the spiritual aspect of life and of nature—of all things—you are sounding a note. And from that centre of wisdom there comes to the soul that wonderful link of love and power. Then you are guided to the right place in the physical life where you can receive the knowledge and the wisdom that you seek. But it depends of course upon the motive of the individual. If that motive is selfless and pure then the individual receives in full measure, *pressed down, and shaken together and running over,* as your Bible says,* the opportunity it seeks. This is the law, the universal and divine law which controls life. On earth people are impatient for this, but when someone passes into spirit life who had such an aspiration, they find themselves with every opportunity to gain knowledge, and to express themselves in art, music and literature. Libraries are always at their disposal. This is what your loved one is able to do when he or she is freed from the limitations of the physical body.

It means nothing to you when we say spirit overcomes space and overcomes time. You see space and time are of the physical state of life. You think in terms of time: how long it takes you to get from A to B, and that gives you an idea of space, because of how long it takes you to get from one to the other. But when you are in the world of spirit you don't have to think in terms of space, travelling from the first sphere of life, for example, to the seventh sphere of life. You are just there by the power of

*Luke 6 : 38

thought. Maybe you are invited there by your guide, or a teacher asks you to come. In a flash you are there.

The Akashic records

When your turn comes to pass to the spirit life, you will in time enter into the halls of learning; and there you will probably commence your education. You will very early in the day be taken into what you might call a cinema, and you will be set before a screen. Upon that screen you will see many pictures thrown—and certainly one of not only the life which you have recently left, but your many lives or past incarnations. You will also see pictures of the happenings on earth thousands and even millions of years ago—events in the history of the earth planet which have played an important part in the evolution of the earth and of the human spirit. You will learn from this display how very brief is the time you know! Indeed you may even learn that time does not exist—all is in the eternal Now.

Thus, you can see, the world also possesses a soul, much as an individual has a soul. In the same fashion that an individual makes his or her karma, and has that karma to account for, so also does he or she share in the nation's karma and in the world's karma. Each nation has its national soul, and there is also a world soul. Therefore you will all someday learn the vital truth that you cannot live looking to yourselves alone, because the records of your lives are always being impressed upon the soul of your nations and also the soul of your world. Therefore every effort made by anyone towards God, towards good, noble and beautiful thought, is raising the soul life of the whole world.

Look at the indescribable and inexplicable beauties of nature. Does not this cause you to think of the immensity of the Intelligence which has created such beauty and perfection? Natural law alone does not account for these. It is natural law which is being directed by divine intelligence. In the same way every minute incident of your life matters—your every thought, word and action—and one day you will be amazed when you have penetrated the iron door of materiality to what lies beyond. For there you will see not only these same thoughts, words and actions thrown upon the etheric screen and sounding from an etheric sound track, but you will know the *effect* all these things made upon the physical universe and upon God's spiritual universe. This is a staggering thought.

Everything you handle is impressed with your etheric emanation. When you enter a room or building, you impress the etheric emanation of that room or building with your own soul substance. As an example, many of you will doubtless have gone into places such as cathedrals. The impressions left behind from the ceremonies there can by very strong, for these etheric impressions are never lost. Your every life, your every past incarnation, is imprinted on the akashic record. This is why a clairvoyant will sometimes be able to tell you about these things, or why you yourself in meditation may rise for a moment to that level of consciousness where you can receive an impression of that past of yours. Sometimes such vision comes only vaguely, in the same way many people experience a feeling when they are visiting a strange place or places that they have been there before. A vague shadowy something makes them say, 'This place is familiar to me'.

Your psychologists explain these matters very readily, but not always correctly. The real explanation lies deeper. People who remember in this fashion touch their akashic record for a flash. Humanity will learn much more than it knows at present about the ancient races and ancient lands. But this will not come from archaeology as you know it; for while archaeology can give a certain amount of help, it will also mislead. Only when humanity has developed the power to receive impressions from the ether will you read the true ancient history of buildings and stones.

Here we come up against suspicion. You dear people are so honest—and that is right—that you do not wish to delude yourselves. You are proud of your reasoning mind. You do not intend to be misled by yourself or by anyone else. Even those who are learning to meditate do not wish to be deluded by what they call 'imagination', by that creative power which is humanity's greatest gift. Be careful, though, lest the lower mind dominates the higher. For if you were bereft of your power to create mind images there would be very little left for you. Have you ever thought that your whole life is directed, your every action urged, through these mental images?

Humanity has to *imagine* clothing, houses, food, agriculture, everything, before bringing it into being. Every activity has first to become in a person's imagination. *Where there is no vision the people perish*, says your Bible.* If there is no power of imagination, of course they must perish. What is vital is that the aspiration of humanity must grow Godward. God is beauty; God creates beauty; God has created people; and through people—God's creation—beauty must become manifest.

This vital subject of your imaginative powers must be deeply studied and far better understood, because imagination is truly the doorway to all your creative powers. It is primarily a spiritual thing and opens up a higher world. As we have said, all your imagining must be pure, beautiful and Godlike. When you are developing these inner powers of your soul, you develop and expand an etheric body, part of which is attached to your outer body, and which interpenetrates your nervous system and your physical makeup. The other portion of your etheric body can

*Proverbs 29 : 18

contact the higher worlds and is akin to your soul. This lower etheric is the bridge between the spirit world and your earth. It dies with your physical body, but not immediately.

The body is finished when spirit and soul are withdrawn; but the lower etheric part lingers for a while and is often seen and described as wraithlike. This also eventually disintegrates. The real and intelligent part of you, the higher etheric, is absorbed into the soul body. This higher body then passes onward, and eventually goes into the light of God. Communications which come through from the spirit world come across an etheric bridge, which is built up by people on earth and by people in the spirit world by their etheric emanations. This is a very delicate structure and easily broken.

A century ago your grandparents would have disbelieved us when we said: 'In the future you will turn a little knob in your home and you will have pictures coming to you from the other side of the world'. They would have thought, 'What utter nonsense!'. And here you are, it is commonplace now! In the world of spirit there are temples of education and there are immense screens, and soul pictures pass across the screen. Many, many things which you would not think possible, such as life on other planets, are reflected on that screen—and also life from ages past when the world was entirely different from what it is today. What do you call it on your earth at the present time? Television. This is the Akashic vision—vision of the Akashic records.

A child's near-death experience—Joyce

I don't know if the 'near-death' experience of a child of seven is of interest to you, although it happened many years ago—I am now over eighty. While undergoing an operation for the removal of tonsils at that age, my heart stopped, I am told. That was not surprising since I was born with a leaking heart valve, and considering the anaesthetics used then. What happened to me while undergoing the operation was this. I found myself coming out of a dark passage into a lovely area of light. I was standing on green grass with a border of flowers as far as I could see. Their colours, because of the wonderful light, were bright but not hurtful. They were colours that I have never seen before or since, and the flowers seemed alive. As I knew that I was still attached to the passage and had to return, I ran round touching them as far as I could reach. There were trees there as well, but the light shone all around. I have tried to draw it many times, but can't.

For years I told everyone what wonderful dreams you have when you have your tonsils out, until I realized it was not an ordinary dream. Now, although passed my eightieth birthday, it is still as clear as the day it happened, and I often return there in meditation.

A brief glimpse beyond the veil—Cynda

I have had several near-death experiences during this incarnation, the most poignant of which occurred in 1955 when my husband and I were on a visit to England from East Africa. We had been in London for only three days when I was suddenly taken ill with intestinal problems and severe abdominal pains. I thought maybe the cause lay in an unfortunate bout of dysentery, but both the doctor and specialist that I visited said that this was not the case, and for all their careful investigations they were unable to diagnose what was wrong with me.

In order to be able to fulfil my commitments I was given painkilling injections and although this was no solution to the problem, I had high hopes that our imminent visit to a Nature Cure Centre might hold the key to a cure for my predicament. Unfortunately, my condition failed to respond to the treatment of 'fasting' prescribed for me and, since conventional medicine was not used in such places and it seemed that the need to call upon the assistance of doctors and nurses was keenly resisted, the situation quickly deteriorated. By the end of the first week, when I had lost two stone in weight and my intake was reduced to a diet of ice-cubes,

204 A GUIDE FOR LIVING WITH DEATH AND DYING

my husband's concern was so great that he forcefully demanded that a trained nurse be brought in.

Her kind ministrations did much to alleviate the pain, but I was now aware that I was slipping in and out of consciousness, until there came that moment when I found myself sitting half way up a mountainside close to a small waterfall. I felt at peace and filled with a sense of freedom as my craving for clear, cool water was at last blissfully soothed. Above me on the mountaintop there stood a glorious Being of Light, shining down upon me with such compassion, his smiling blue eyes filled with love. His arms were spread wide and the huge aura around him encircled him in violet light, giving me the impression of a cross of light within a circle of light: a powerful symbol of which I was not fully aware at that time. I longed to go to him but he did not beckon me. Instead, he pointed a finger towards the foot of the mountain. I turned my head and saw (as though looking through a window) a picture of myself lying on a bed surrounded by several men, a nurse and my dear husband who was leaning over me and kissing my cheek as he rhythmically repeated, 'I love you darling, I love you darling'.

I was so deeply moved by this loving gesture—so alien to his usual, shy, reserved nature when in the presence of others—that I knew I could not leave this beloved man who meant so much to me. The time was not right: I had to go back. Immediately the decision was made I found myself back in that painful body. The healing process was almost instantaneous and I made a remarkable recovery, though it was never discovered exactly what it was that nearly took me away from the earth plane.

In retrospect, I believe that beautiful Being of Light was White Eagle and that the message he conveyed was understood by my higher self and obeyed.

Animals after death

People can feel great sorrow when a pet dies, and there are different thoughts about what happens to an animal then. White Eagle is reassuring about this, and the last words quoted here are ones which are often sent from the White Eagle Lodge to people who ask for help with their sadness over such a loss. First, however, White Eagle helps us to understand the difference between human and animal consciousness.

God-consciousness is not found in the lower forms of life. People argue but cannot decide as to whether the animal has any consciousness of the divine. Yes, the domestic animal, by its devotion to people, is developing a higher consciousness; but we, who can observe all the steps of its evolution in physical matter, have yet to discern any divine consciousness in animals. You must remember, however, that all animals, even in the wild, can be influenced by the divine spirit *through humans*. Because of this, humanity has a grave and great responsibility towards the animal kingdom. The domestic animal, and even wild animals, do indeed recognize that divine quality of love in a man or woman. But not all people have this divine quality. Many people are cruel to animals because they do not comprehend the meaning of divine love. Consequently, the wild animal must defend itself because its animal instinct tells it to. The domestic animal is devoted to and trusts the people from whom it receives food, its comfortable home, warmth and protection. Nevertheless, we cannot say that the animal has as yet any consciousness of divinity or of eternal life; but you can still help the animal on its evolutionary path.

What is the difference, then, between a man or woman and the animal? It is in the former's consciousness, in his or her soul-qualities. Undoubtedly our little friend the animal has also certain soul-qualities and develops a character. That is why many people will meet their animal friends again after death. Sad to relate, they will also have to face any cruelty they have inflicted upon any other animals during their earth life. For at some time, either on the astral or again on the physical plane, all cruelty committed by human beings has to be faced and eradicated.

The difference, therefore, between animal life and the consciousness of humanity is this. At a certain stage a person awakens
to awareness of the divine within him or her. You will say that
many humans seem to be little better, and in some instances far
below a highly sensitized and developed animal. In those people
there is, at the moment, no God-consciousness. And that state
can and does also exist in the apparently clever type of person,
the one with a highly-developed intellect.

There are, in history, teachings that we have evolved from animals, and
that an individual soul can become an animal again. It comes out as a
fear, sometimes, as in the question which follows. The tone of White
Eagle's answer suggests that he understood that fear. The questioner
asked, referring to a well-known Spiritualist account of Jesus' life, 'Jesus
said in the Aquarian Gospel that we never have been animal, but always
spirit. You say the animal line is a different line of evolution?'. 'Beloved',
replied White Eagle, 'You can never be less than you are. God has always
been in man, in woman. You have always had God within you, but this
has awaited a development into full consciousness, full power'.

We understand the pain of parting with a visible form. We can
say little to comfort those who have parted with the physical form
of their beloved pet, but we can give you this picture. Your little
pet is bounding through fields and gardens in the heavenly life.
Your pet is so happy with his or her companions and is quite
unaware that he or she is not with you, for at night your soul goes
to be with your pet, and is with you in happy companionship. It
is true. Your night is day to your pet, and your day on earth is
night. Hold this picture, and be thankful for the joy of your pet,
who is not dead, but lives always in God's kingdom.

As you develop this higher consciousness of soul you will
know that you cannot be separated from loved ones, whether
they are animal or human.

Cats, transition and reincarnation—Dickie

Leo and Pin came to us as kittens as soon as they were able to leave their mother. As they grew up, they invented all sorts of games. There was a particular one at bed time when they would chase each other all around the drawing room, over the furniture, sofa, chairs and tables; then out into the hall, pursuing each other up the stairs, and finish with a rough and tumble under our bed. As time went on Leo grew very big and strong. Pin could only knock him over by surprising him when he was looking the other way. Then she had kittens (including Bella), which gave her other things to think about. Later she lost an eye, which caused her great distress, and the game stopped.

Two years on Pamela and I had just gone to bed, when all of a sudden we heard what seemed to be the old game start downstairs. Sure enough, there came the thunder of galloping paws up the stairs, into our room, and under the bed. The light had already been turned out, so we did not actually see them come in, but there was no doubt about what was happening: for the first time for years, the game was in progress again. We switched on a bedside lamp, the noise subsided, and a very puzzled Leo eventually came out all by himself. Pin did not seem to be there. Pin had been killed instantly and painlessly by a car on the main road within the previous half hour, we think. She had emerged, achieved her orientation, found the she had two eyes again, and delighted, she had come rushing indoors to bounce Leo!

My cat Blackie was probably closer to me than any of the others; she used to climb on to my shoulders and clean my back hair with her tongue! Her kidneys failed when she was sixteen years old, so we helped her over. Forty-eight hours afterwards, she came stepping proudly through the bedroom door in an aura of golden light. Her eyes were a beautiful gold; she had a black, glossy coat and was so smug at being big and strong again.

XI. RETURNING CONSCIOUSNESS

LIFE—ALL OUR life, whether on earth or at other levels—is a process of returning more and more into a complete consciousness. We return to awareness of consciousness on the physical plane as we are born again in matter, and we return to awareness of layers of broader consciousness than the physical when we die. Our life's purpose is to return to an awareness of spiritual consciousness throughout all our being and at all levels.

Non-consciousness rarely happens, but during earthly life we are often unaware that we are conscious as a spiritual being, and so we fear to die, little realizing that when we die we reconnect with a much more alive part of ourselves than we know while on earth! This is why spiritual teachers like White Eagle promote meditation, contemplation, prayer, entering the silence and mindfulness. They know that if we can get a glimpse of our own spiritual level of consciousness while on earth, it will transform our lives from fear to trust; and in the process we will reach that fountain of Christ love within our self which is a never-ending source of strength and wisdom. The Christ love is a spontaneous outpouring of kindness and love towards all life.

One of the purposes of this book, and of White Eagle's teaching, has been to focus upon this broader vision of consciousness. We hope his teaching on the subject may have brought comfort and hope at quite a personal level to those who are bereaved or frightened of dying, and alleviated some of their sadness, fear and pain. For those who are caregivers working with people who are approaching their transition, we hope that this book may give the emotional strength to continue with your loving service with a peaceful mind, and not to be overwhelmed by the amount of suffering you witness. We hope White Eagle's words will prevent in everyone that most debilitating of feelings: despair.

For those of you who are confronting death yourself, be reassured. In some ways you are in the best position, because when the moment comes you will find the truth of what White Eagle says before you. You will find yourself with dear ones you thought gone forever. You will be surrounded and filled with feelings of peace and love and comfort which you may never have had in this life. You will know that those who remain on earth are still close to you, and you will meet with them when they sleep. You will see the broader picture and reconnect with a greater whole—a self which is all you know you can be. You will instantly understand and then forget the pain you may now be in, and the compensation for it will be overwhelmingly beautiful. You will feel as if you still have a body, but one which is doing what you want it to do. You will be able to run, dance, swim, even fly, and go—instantly if you wish—to all those places and memories both on earth and elsewhere which you long to visit, or revisit. And you will be happy, for as White Eagle says at the end of THE QUIET MIND, 'Happiness is the realization of God in the heart'; and at the moment you die you will know the truth of God.

Why we return

White Eagle was asked about the soul returning to earth after it had reached the heaven world.

It is a natural question; when you think of your beloved friends passing from earth, or returning to you from time to time bearing messages and descriptions of the heavenly places in which they live, it makes you wonder why that soul, having been released, must be drawn back again? There seems no sense in it. If the soul can climb to heaven and absorb there so much of the glory of the light, it seems inconceivable for such a soul to retrace its steps and be reborn in lowly or perhaps uncongenial conditions in the earth life. It seems a transgression of the divine order of love and progress.

Let us first of all consider a human life of 'threescore years

AFFIRMATIONS FOR AWAKENING, AND A MEDITATION

◊   I breathe in peace; I breathe out love.

◊   I am safe; all is well.

◊   I let go, and open my heart and mind to receive healing.

◊   I am spirit, and spirit is eternal.

◊   Within me is the Christ light which can overcome all ...... (fear, pain, sorrow, guilt, illusion, confusion etc.)

◊   I am surrounded by loving help.

◊   Death is an awakening to a more beautiful life.

◊   I can lose nothing and no-one; I will always be in touch with those I love.

◊   This moment is perfect, and from it I can grow in ...... (peace, love, strength, well-being, joy etc.)

◊   In my darkest moments I am closest to God.

◊   My spirit is strong, and knows my need; all is as it should be.

◊   I can trust myself.

◊   My body is only part of me; I live beyond it.

◊   I surrender to the rightness of this moment.

◊   The power of God upholds me; there is nothing to fear.

◊   I am more than this pain.

◊   My loving, listening presence is powerful, and just what is needed.

◊   I release my feelings of .....(fear, anger, hurt, resentment, bitterness, depair etc.); I breathe in love.

◊   God's love is unconditional; I am safe.

◊   I inwardly release my loved one, knowing we will never be parted.

◊   I go forward into the Light with joy.

The following passage from White Eagle's teaching also forms another beautiful meditation to use.

'Sitting in the silence, relax and breathe in the fragrance of the rose. Breathe in the light of God. Breathe out the love of God. Be still and know God. Be calm, be tranquil, dear children, and you will be happy.

'You must find the secret of happiness yourself before you can impart it to others. Yet, sorrow is akin to happiness. Out of present sorrow and grief will be born joy and happiness. Happiness will as surely follow sorrow as day follows night.

'The Brethren bless you and tenderly love you. Think of their love for you and it will help you upwards. They know your need; the supply is limitless.'

and ten'. Although it may be only three days, three months or three years, or well over that biblical span, let us consider that one physical span of birth, life, and then death. Let us then compare any ordinary decent man or woman with the glorious expression of godliness of one of the great teachers or masters. How do you account for the difference?

How does the radiant soul become radiant? Through the discipline of the physical life. Discipline spells growth, and the finest discipline ordained by God is what your poet calls 'the trivial round, the common task'.*

And yet every human soul struggles against it. You will say 'Yes, we can accept that; but does not the soul have opportunities on the astral plane for development?'. To a certain degree; but remember that the limitations of time and space, the restrictions of physical life are removed in the next plane of life. Therefore there cannot be discipline of the same nature in the beyond as on the physical plane. So the purpose of reincarnation is discipline for the spirit or ego.

Remember that while the work of the soul may go on after death, nevertheless special opportunities are given to you while on earth to bring through and develop the God-consciousness. You may prefer to call it the cosmic consciousness or the Christ consciousness. But that consciousness *must be brought through into physical life.*

Special opportunities are presented to you in your outer form to develop and grow in this God-consciousness. This is the reason why, when you have lost your physical body and you awaken to a heavenly state of awareness, you see how you have neglected to take advantage of opportunities afforded by the earth life. That is when your soul begins to feel an urge and desire to return again to earth, where fresh opportunities await it.

*The quotation is from John Keble's hymn, 'New every morning'.

Many say, 'When I get to heaven I shall not want to come back to earth—I don't see any need to do so!'. No, you do not see the need now, but when you catch a glimpse of the glories of God's life, God's heavenly manifestation, God's beauty, you may do. When the soul is able to look into its inmost depth and see the potential beauty and good therein, then the soul desires only one thing, to purify and perfect itself. It cries out, 'How can I be more worthy to look upon such glory?'.

The path is indicated. There is only one way and that is through work. So the soul descends and takes on another life on earth, for the soul has heard—ringing through the temple above, ringing through the Temple of the Silence—the words, 'Let the Light Shine'.

White Eagle was asked another question about previous lives: 'When you go into the spirit world, can you see all your lives, so that you know how far you have progressed?' His answer was interesting and salutary.

We must be very careful. When you get to the spirit world you go through a school. You enter the kindergarten, and then you rise up through the planes. As you rise up, you shed a little of your earthiness, just as the physical body formerly fell away. You rise in spiritual understanding until you are shown the whole picture. You see yourself as you really are. *For now we see through a glass, darkly; but then face to face.* In other words, the soul looks upon the glory of God and sees itself in comparison. It knows then there is only one thing it wants: to be able to get nearer to God and to be purified and perfected; to become made perfect in the image of God, even as Christ who is the Son of God.

When the soul has reached that stage there are guides, teachers and helpers ready. 'You require to learn certain lessons, my brother, my sister', the voice says. 'This life will bring you into contact with this or that soul, with whom you have contracted a karmic debt.' Alternative paths are shown, too. The soul can choose which one it takes. There are many, many opportunities that the soul has of working out its salvation. You find it difficult to believe that your troubles, as you call them, are of your own making? Your nose is too close to the picture. Nevertheless, the pattern of your life is something you have made for yourself, by your past actions and because of your spiritual aspiration. So you get two pulls. There is that of your past karma, which is what one might call the negative; and that of your spiritual aspiration, the pull of your soul to God. But over all these conditions, love is the ruler. We hope this has answered your question.

Let us now consider the true home of the soul. The true home of the soul is in the celestial, a place of beauty and bliss. When young souls enter such a condition they may be likened to babes lying in the womb. They are conscious of the glory of God, but they have yet to learn to use their limbs, to kick, to walk and to act. Let us remember also that those young babes are young Gods—young creators. Your creator, God, devised the means of physical existence as a form of discipline to train that child to use its faculties—not primarily the physical faculties, but the *God-faculties*. Now, when the babe returns to the earth plane, it brings with it a certain amount of consciousness, God-consciousness. It may pass through the discipline of the physical life, eagerly absorbing its lessons; it may return to its home with an abundant harvest, in which case that particular life will stand out as a most important one. Against this the soul may only mark time, or take only a few tottering steps forward and return with but a tiny sheaf. When the soul returns thus to its home after it has shed its outer vehicles of manifestation, the lower sheaths, there does not remain a very great deal from that one particular incarnation.

In dealing with your earth companions, remember they are

not all Mr Smith or Mrs Patel, but living souls. They may have been anything in a former life—you do not know. If you could only cultivate the vision to see beneath the personality, in order to get to the soul, then you would not object to the truth of reincarnation.

It has been said by some teachers that reincarnation is an illusion. Previous lives come into being and pass. In a sense such lives *are* illusory, and yet they are a reality. A paradox. But when you have reached beyond the personality and touched reality, you will see what we mean when we say that reincarnation is illusion. It is because all lies in the present—there is no past, all is present; in that sense reincarnation is an illusion. And yet the discipline of the soul is brought over to and remains in the heaven world.

White Eagle was further asked, 'Is it possible for a soul to become spiritually developed in one incarnation, but come back to earth with that part of itself shut away, or with the blinds down, as you put it?'. He replied:

It may be necessary for a soul to come back in a certain incarnation with other qualities of character more prominent, because he or she may have service to give, for instance at a more material level. If this service to humanity takes the person into a commercial walk of life, it will be necessary for commercial instincts and gifts to take full play. The light from heaven would rather dazzle and divert the soul from its course. So the light is mercifully veiled for the time being. This will indicate how impossible it is for anyone to judge another soul.

The questioner asked further: 'Will the spiritual consciousness return to this soul? Is that how you would explain cases of sudden conversion or illumination?'. And White Eagle's reply was this.

When the soul has accomplished the specific work it needed to so, and learnt the lesson, it is quite likely that the spiritual light will flood the higher consciousness to such a degree that his or her ordinary consciousness becomes aware of it.

Beloved brethren, one and all, we come to you in these earth conditions, with one hope, and it is this: to bring love, so that love may help you to understand some of your many problems. All that we have said comes with deep love and understanding of your human difficulties. We know also that the solution of all human difficulties comes when love and brotherhood, compassion and sympathy, take the place of the outer judgment of our brother, our sister. Let us all continue to strive for this greater brotherhood and greater love, and increasing wisdom.

White Eagle has talked often about how we reincarnate in groups: souls drawn together by ties of emotion, by individual karma and the karma of the group as a whole. People will be in different relationships and of different genders within the group each time, but they will move on together, growing in love and wisdom. This is also true of groups meeting to give spiritual service, which are the starting point for the next passage. Apart from the short meditation which comes after, we end this book with this passage because it presents a rounded and inspiring picture of continuity throughout all levels of life. The 'illumined ones' White Eagle refers to are those who have transcended the limitations of materi-ality completely, through many lives on earth, and are now helping us, their younger brethren, to do likewise. We hope that this passage, however brief, will open the consciousness to new possibilities.

Do you feel the presence of the brethren of the Sun, the illumined ones? So many times have we met together, you and we, not only in those days of Atlantis in the temples there, but also as Native Americans. These people were the children of the people of Atlantis. We used to go to the hilltops and watch the rising sun together; we used to bow down and worship the setting sun. We would not be together here in the White Eagle Lodge were we not impelled by ties and links of the past. This is what we mean by the drawing together of groups and families again and again and again. What beautiful provision by our Father–Mother God! We come back life after life until we are all welded together and absorbed into the eternal Sun, not to lose our individuality, but for each one of us to expand in consciousness and become as the sons and daughters of God.

THE LAKE OF PEACE

Arise out of yourself,
Let go the garment of the body:
Seek the place of healing silence and tranquillity,
Seek the lake of peace within,
Calm and tideless.
Let the boat of the mind glide slowly
        from its moorings
(Leave the turbulent, restless river)
Past the soft green fingers of the rushes,
Into the lake's cool silver,
Quiet rippling at the prow.
Here the unruffled heart must wait.
Wait not impatiently for the long-sought action,
The eager self outstretched to grasp
And to hold tightly.
Wait gently—as the water waits
For the cool touch of light upon its
        moving stillness,
For the pulse of the evening air—
Steadily beating.

There is calm here and awareness of nature,
So be tranquil and aware of God.
Though the hand of time is still closed to
        your desires,
Let go desire for it is the measure of your
        uncertainty,
Your lack of faith.
By the clear light of aspiration
You shall see:
You shall see there is peace in acceptance
That His will may be done.
Rest in the timeless centre of your being,
The dwelling place of wisdom.
When you are ready
The appointed hour shall come.

                                        T.D.

BIBLIOGRAPHY

White Eagle publications, published by the White Eagle Publishing Trust, including those mentioned in the text. The place of publication is Liss, Hants. In particular note SUNRISE *and the tape* BRIDGE TO THE WORLD OF LIGHT.

THE GENTLE BROTHER. 1968, second edition 1999, ISBN 0-85487-112-8

THE LIVING WORD OF ST JOHN. 1949, third edition 2000, ISBN 0-85487-23-3

MEDITATION. 1955, third edition 1999, ISBN 0-85487-110-1

FIRST STEPS ON A SPIRITUAL PATH (MORNING LIGHT). 2005, ISBN 0-85487-162-4

PRAYER, MINDFULNESS AND INNER CHANGE (PRAYER IN THE NEW AGE). 1957, reissued under the new title 2003, ISBN 0-85487-144-6

THE SOURCE OF ALL OUR STRENGTH. 1996, second edition 1999, ISBN 0-85487-117-9

THE STILL VOICE. 1981, ISBN 0-85487-049-0

THE PATH OF THE SOUL. 1959, second edition 1997, ISBN 0-85487-101-2

THE QUIET MIND. 1972, second edition 1998, ISBN 0-85487-104-7

SUNRISE. 1958, second edition 2001, ISBN 0-85487-114-4

WALKING WITH THE ANGELS. 1998, ISBN 0-85487-109-8

ALL IS WELL (relaxation tape)

BRIDGE TO THE WORLD OF LIGHT (tape)

Books on grieving and death, general books, and books on counselling

THE COURAGE TO GRIEVE. Judy Tatelbaum, second edition, 1993, ISBN 0749309369

ON CHILDREN AND DEATH. Elisabeth Kübler-Ross, revised edition 1997, ISBN 0684839393

ON DEATH AND DYING. Elisabeth Kübler-Ross, 1973, ISBN 0415040159

DEATH THE FINAL STAGE OF GROWTH. Elisabeth Kübler-Ross, revised edition 1997, ISBN 0684839415

LIFE AFTER LIFE. Raymond Moody, 1976, 2001, ISBN 0712602739

EMMANUEL'S BOOK III: WHAT IS AN ANGEL DOING HERE? Compiled by Pat Rodegast and Judith Stanton, 1994, ISBN 0-553-37412-5

THE TAO OF LEADERSHIP. John Heider, 1986, ISBN 0893340790

THEY WALKED WITH JESUS. Dolores Cannon,1994, ISBN 1-85860-007-3

THE DANCING WU LI MASTERS. Gary Zukav, 1979, ISBN 0-00-654030-9

EMBRACED BY THE LIGHT. Betty J. Eadie, 1992, ISBN 1-85538-439-6

HEALING CONVERSATIONS: WHAT TO SAY WHEN YOU DON'T KNOW WHAT TO SAY. Nance Guilmartin, 2002, ISBN 0787960195

TESTIMONY OF LIGHT. Helen Greaves, revised edition 1977, ISBN 0854351647

THE TAO OF PHYSICS. Fritjov Capra, 1976 ISBN 0-00-654023-6

THE TIBETAN BOOK OF LIVING AND DYING. Sogyal Rinpoche, 1992 ISBN 0-7126-7139-0

RETURN FROM DEATH: AN EXPLORATION OF THE NEAR-DEATH EXPERIENCE. Margot Grey, 1985, ISBN 1-85063-019-4

ON BECOMING A COUNSELLOR. Eugene Kennedy, 1977, revised edition 2002, ISBN 0717133478

WHAT TO DO WHEN YOU ARE DEAD. Craig Hamilton-Parker, 2002, ISBN 0806929960

BIBLICAL REFERENCES

References to stories and sayings in the Bible, when not given in the text or footnotes. All are to the King James (1611) version.
Page 15 (many mansions): John 14 : 2. Page 23 (the prince of this world): John 14 : 30. Page 24 (more blessed to give): Acts 20 : 35. Page 25 (Whither I go): John 13 : 36. Page 26 (the miraculous draft of fishes): John 21. Page 49 (I am the resurrection): John 11 : 25. Page 87 (I am with you alway): Matthew 28 : 20. Page 89 (lest thou dash thy foot): Matthew 4 : 6. Page 91 (Love the Lord thy God): Matthew 22 : 37–39. Page 125 (Sell all that thou hast): Luke 18 : 22. Page 146 (the very hairs of your head): Matthew 10 : 29–30. Page 148 (taken away my Lord): John 20 : 13. Page 168 (stone rolled away): John 20 : 1. Page 173 (Touch me not): John 20 : 17. Page 212 (through a glass, darkly): I Corinthians 13 : 12.

INDEX